The
TRUTH
ABOUT THE
SHROUD
of TURIN

SOLVING THE MYSTERY

ROBERT K. WILCOX

Since 1947
**REGNERY
PUBLISHING, INC.**
An Eagle Publishing Company • Washington, DC

Library of Congress Cataloging-in-Publication Data

Wilcox, Robert K.
  The truth about the Shroud of Turin : solving the mystery / by Robert K.
Wilcox.
      p. cm.
  Includes bibliographical references and index.
  ISBN 978-1-59698-600-8 (alk. paper)
  1. Holy Shroud. I. Title.
  BT587.S4W513 2010
  232.96'6—dc22

                                        2009046078

Published in the United States by

Regnery Publishing, Inc.
One Massachusetts Avenue, NW
Washington, DC 20001
www.regnery.com

Manufactured in the United States of America

10 9 8 7 6 5 4 3 2 1

Books are available in quantity for promotional or premium use. Write to
Director of Special Sales, Regnery Publishing, Inc., One Massachusetts
Avenue NW, Washington, DC 20001, for information on discounts and
terms or call (202) 216-0600.

Distributed to the trade by:
Perseus Distribution
387 Park Avenue South
New York, NY 10016

The
TRUTH
ABOUT THE
SHROUD
of TURIN

To Ama

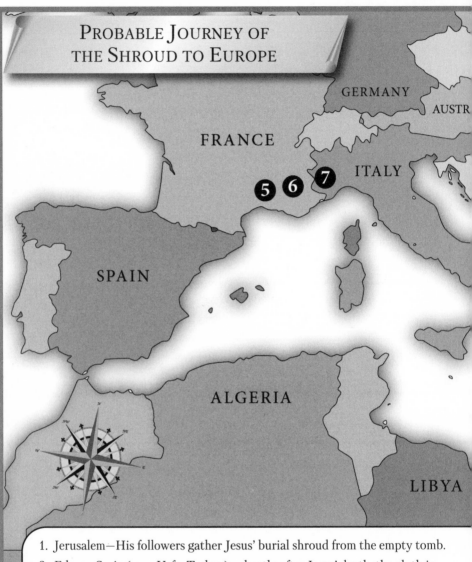

PROBABLE JOURNEY OF THE SHROUD TO EUROPE

GERMANY

AUSTR

FRANCE

ITALY

5 **6** **7**

SPAIN

ALGERIA

LIBYA

1. Jerusalem—His followers gather Jesus' burial shroud from the empty tomb.

2. Edessa, Syria (now Urfa, Turkey)—shortly after Jesus' death, the cloth is transported here. In 525, following a devastating flood, it is found sealed in an Edessan city wall.

3. 943—Venerated as the "Cloth of Edessa" or "Mandylion," the shroud is ransomed from Muslim captors and brought triumphantly to Constantinople (now Istanbul, Turkey).

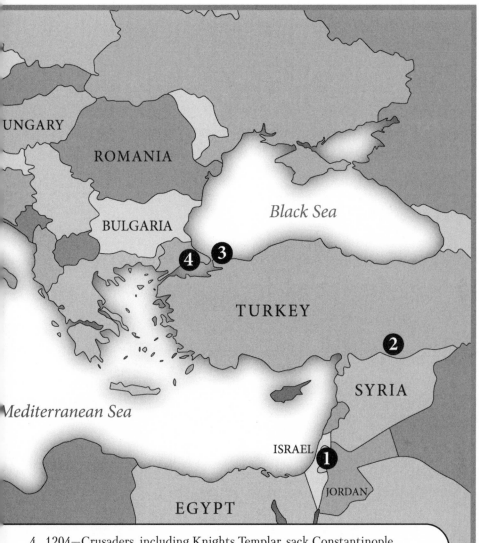

4. 1204—Crusaders, including Knights Templar, sack Constantinople. The shroud disappears.

5. 1355—The cloth is displayed publicly in a church in Lirey, France, owned by Geoffrey de Charny, probably a descendent of Templar Geoffrey I de Charny.

6. 1502—The shroud is moved to Chambery, France.

7. 1578—The shroud is taken to Turin, Italy, where it now resides.

CONTENTS

PART III: 2010, THE MYSTERY CONTINUES

PREFACE

Since I first began to investigate the shroud of Turin in 1973, much has happened. Over the last four decades we have seen the shroud allegedly debunked by Carbon 14 dating only to have the debunking debunked by later analysis. We have now seen new mysteries discovered on the shroud. For instance, the body images have a quality called "3-Dimensionality," found only in photographs of deep space. And now we even have a probable link between the shroud and the Knights Templar, which fills in the most important blank in the history of the shroud.

All these discoveries, and more, as well as the 2010 rare public exposition of the linen, prompted me to renew my investigation and write the book you have before you. The shroud of Turin is, to my mind, the most fascinating Christian relic in existence—the alleged burial cloth of Christ, bearing an apparently inexplicable, even supernatural, image which many believe to be that of the historical figure of Jesus of Nazareth after his crucifixion.

Many have tried to explain the shroud from a purely natural level—and some of these natural explanations can sound more outlandish than miracles. But in this book I try to give every theory its due and let you, the reader, decide how the evidence stacks up. You must be the judge. It's a wild ride, an important ride. The shroud of Turin traverses much of western history and, if authentic, could have startling implications.

I come at this subject as a reporter. I've been one for the *New York Times*, the *Miami Herald*, and the *Catholic Digest*, among others. I know, from my own sifting of the evidence, what I think to be true. But this book is not an attempt to present you with my opinions as fact. It is an attempt to present a true portrait of one of the most breathtaking relics of the past—whether one thinks that past takes us into the shop of a medieval forger or to a burial ground in the Holy Land.

In 1973, I did the leg work, traveling the world, photographing the shroud, and sitting down with and interviewing many of the experts who had devoted their professional lives to studying it and its mysteries. Since then I've taken a different investigative approach, analyzing the material more as a scholar would—though I confess immediately that I am not an expert in either Carbon 14 dating, or weaving, or the burial rites of the Jews of New Testament times, or many other disciplines relevant to the ancient linen. But what I can bring to bear is a long association with the subject, a reporter's nose for the facts, story-telling ability—and make no mistake, authentic or not, the shroud is a monster story—and the weight of judgment that comes from experience.

It is has been a great adventure for me to re-immerse myself in this compelling story—a mystery that is arguably one of the most important that anyone can possibly want to solve. For me, given the fact that I began my book-writing career with the shroud, and am still devoting such effort to the relic, it has been a personal quest—a quest taking me back over 2,000 years of history, and forward into Space Age science. I hope you find this as interesting and exciting a detective story as I do.

—Robert K. Wilcox
Los Angeles, California
January 25, 2010

PART I
1898 – 1902

■■■■■■■■

THE
PHOTOGRAPH

CHAPTER 1

■■■■■■■■

A STARTLING DISCOVERY

Secondo Pia souped his negative, waiting for the large glass plate to develop. The 42-year-old Italian lawyer, small town mayor, and amateur photographer had had a rough time photographing the Holy Shroud of Turin, believed by most in his native Northern Italy to be the burial cloth of Christ. Photography was new and little understood. Some, especially in the Church, were suspicious of the process. Equipment, heavy and unwieldy, frequently broke down. Electricity for his powerful arc lights had been erratic.

But he had persisted. And now, in his eerily lit darkroom, he was about to get the surprise of his life.

It was just past midnight, May 29, the third day of the first public exposition of the Shroud since 1868—as always, a rare occasion, this being the 50th anniversary of the signing of the

Italian constitution. He'd been asked to make the photographs by the king himself.

He felt privileged.

The shroud he labored over was made of ivory-colored, almost yellow linen, and was disfigured in several distinct ways. Wrinkles zig-zagged the 14 ½-foot length and 3 ½-foot width of the cloth whenever it was hung for exposition. Burn marks from a fire in 1532 ran down the cloth's sides. Water marks resembling rough-cut diamonds, made when the sixteenth-century fire was doused, could be seen with the naked eye.

Also appearing on the shroud were two softly diffused but distinct impressions of a body. They were difficult to see up close, but at a distance they stood out in subtle, very light brown. It was as though the cloth had been wrapped around a body—not in mummy fashion, but lengthwise—beginning at the heels and proceeding up the back to the base of the skull, then over the head, across the face, and down to the toes.

The face was owl-like, almost grotesque. The eyes were open and staring, with what looked like pinholes for pupils. The nose was long and thin—a line in the center of the face. The mouth was a smudge beneath the nostrils. The hair appeared coarse and stringy, and hung almost to the neck in what appeared to be two braids. Between the hair and the sides of the face was a curious space. The feet appeared to be missing from the frontal image, and the legs were little more than lines tapering from the trunk. But the thighs, knees, and calves could be discerned, and the hands were folded over the loins in repose. The stomach, chest, and arms were easily recognizable on the frontal image, whereas the head, shoulders, and buttocks stood out on the dorsal.

The dull red stain of blood was everywhere. Large droplets from under the hairline suggested the entrance points of thorn-like instruments. Small lacerations all over the body could easily have been the result of indiscriminate and interminable flogging. Wounds from nails resulted in large seepages on the hands as well as thin trickles on the arms. The gash in the side showed the most bleeding; blood had gathered around the hole and then flowed down the sides of the body and across the small of the back.

These were the images Secondo Pia expected to see as he waited for the negative to develop. But what he saw as he held the dripping plate up to the red light was something far different. The face was alive with expression, its details almost portrait-like. The eyes were closed and tranquil as though the figure were asleep. The mouth was full, with mustache above and beard below. The nose was long and prominent, with gradations of shadow down the sides. The hair, strands of which were matted with blood, appeared soft and smooth.

What Pia was looking at—inexplicably—were *positive* images. So what he saw on the cloth itself, the photographer concluded, must be *negative* images. Exactly how this strange reversal had been transferred to the shroud he could not say. What was clear, at least to Pia, was that Jesus had left not only his "photograph" on the shroud, but also a visual record of what happened to him in the bloody hours before his death.

■ ■ ■ ■ ■ ■ ■ ■

News of Pia's startling discovery was not immediately released to the press. It was decided to keep things quiet until more study could be made.

However, three days later, Turin's *Corriere Nazionale*, apparently scoring a leak, reported: "The photography was stupendously successful. It represents an exceptional value to history, science and religion." Soon the *London Daily Telegraph* gushed: "The rumor of the marvelous event spread like wildfire in Turin. His Grace the Archbishop, Duchess Isabella, Princess Clara, illustrious prelates, artists and businessmen hastened to Signor Pia's studio to investigate the truth of the rumours. . . ." Pia was said to have set up his negatives with bright lights behind them in order for dignitaries being ushered into the darkened parlor to better see the stupendous sight.

By June 15, the Vatican's official newspaper, *L'Osservatore Romano*, was calling Pia's discovery a "miraculous event."

That endorsement sent the story global.

At first, reports in world capitals were favorable. But then problems peculiar to 1898 arose. Photographs could not yet be transmitted by wire. Newspapers commissioned artists to make drawings of Pia's photos, a decision that negated the photographic revelation.

At least one newspaper photographed an ancient painting of the shroud and ran it as what Pia had produced. So numerous were the number of "misleading reproductions from sketches, etc., published in lay journals," wrote the editor of *The Photogram*, a leading British technical magazine, that he included a written guarantee from Pia that the photos in his 1898 Christmas shroud supplement were authentic.

General lack of knowledge about photography also took its toll. Papers, already hampered by a serious information dearth, garbled what little they had. According to John Walsh, an American author who researched the reaction in his 1963 book *The Shroud*, the June 26, 1898, issue of *The New York Evening Journal* "managed to include both enough untruth and distortion in both word and picture, to cause hopeless confusion." The *Journal's* full-page display was illustrated by prominent artist A. Bianchini, whose sketches, Walsh wrote, were "almost incomprehensibly bad." Such presentation, however, probably made little difference. Americans were embroiled in the Spanish-American War, and their attention was largely on Cuba.

Even reports correctly stating the scientific mystery were hampered because of their overly pious emotion. "Nothing is more attractive than the countenance, truly divine," invoked the *Photogram*. "The mouth . . . appears to exhale the last sigh of Him who was obedient even to the death." The negative "has left us . . . the memorial of His Passion, His Death, and His Glorious Resurrection."

Such devotion alienated those who considered themselves enlightened. This was the dawn of the twentieth century. Religion and science were often at odds. Actual distance from Turin—a city half a world away from, for instance, New York City—muddled things further. These were not days of instant communication. Acceptance turned first to hesitancy, then to hostility towards Pia. He was accused of chicanery with chemicals, doctoring the negatives, even blunderingly photographing the wrong side of the shroud, a charge that failed to recognize that it had a prohibiting red silk backing attached.

> ### Pia's Photos of the Holy Face
>
> Secondo Pia's photograph became an integral part of the Catholic devotion to the Holy Face of Jesus, which was just starting to take hold in Italy in the nineteenth century.

Feeling a need to defend himself, Pia wrote two memoirs, the last of which was published in 1907. "I never invented any new methods or utilized any tricks as some people have been inclined to believe," he said. "I had had long practice as an amateur photographer, and had been used to all kinds of adverse conditions."

Pia listed his technical data: he had used a Voigtlander lens with a seven millimeter aperture opening, and standard 2, 3½ x 1,

6½-inch isochromatic negative plates developed in iron oxalate solution fixed with hyposulphite. He concluded, "On my honor I assure you, neither the negatives nor the copies from it were ever retouched. . . . Some rushed to conclusions without knowledge. . . . They ignored the special difficulties I faced. . . . I am confident that my declaration can destroy their unfounded hypotheses. This will defend—along with other experts—the honesty that inspired my task."

But before the memoirs were ever published, a churchman, ironically, had sounded the death knell for the shroud.

THE D'ARCIS MEMORANDUM

Father Ulysee Chevalier, a French historian and debunker of relics, had followed the Turin controversy with interest. He was hard at work on a massive bibliography of ancient sources that would soon bring him international fame. Titled *Repertoire des sources historiques du moyan age*, the work strove to list the names and sources of almost every notable person in literature since the time of Christ. Among the documents he'd encountered in his research were a batch written around 1389, some thirty-five years *after* the shroud had first surfaced in a Crusader knight's castle in Lirey, France. That mysterious surfacing had been in 1354. Before 1354, the shroud's history was obscure, and it was generally believed that the linen, venerated at least in Lirey as Christ's own burial cloth, was a spoil of war from the Holy Land.

But Chevalier's 1389 documents called the shroud a painted fake. Chief among these documents was an essay entitled "The D'Arcis Memorandum." "D'Arcis" was Bishop Pierre D'Arcis, head prelate of Lirey, who, in 1389, was angered that Geoffrey DeCharny, the son of the Crusader knight of the same name, had begun exhibiting the linen as the True Shroud. D'Arcis alleged his predecessor, Bishop Henry of Poitiers, had investigated the shroud thirty-five years earlier and found its forger. "After diligent inquiry and examination," D'Arcis wrote, Bishop Poitiers had "discovered the fraud and how the said cloth had been cunningly painted, the truth being attested by the artist who had painted it, to wit, that it was a work of human skill and not miraculously wrought or bestowed. . . . "

DeCharny and his priests were deceiving the populace, charged D'Arcis. He wanted it stopped. He sent the memorandum and supporting papers to Clement VII, the Avignon Pope who had jurisdiction, hoping Clement would agree. But there was nothing else in the memorandum or accompanying papers about the alleged forger—not his name or his method. D'Arcis' case, in effect, was hearsay. While Clement ordered DeCharny to label the shroud only a "replica" of Christ's burial cloth, he also harshly reprimanded D'Arcis, telling him to stop fighting with those at Lirey, or be excommunicated, leaving thus the impression that D'Arcis himself might be faking.

But the documents were enough for Chevalier. He was not concerned with the positive-negative anomaly or Clement's sanctioning of D'Arcis. In 1900, he published his opinion that the Turin Shroud was an artist's fake. The article was entitled "Critical Study on the Origins of the Holy Shroud of Lirey-Chambery-Turin." Almost immediately Chevalier was deluged with public acclaim. Leopold Delisle, Frances's most celebrated historian, publicly endorsed Chevalier's finding. The Academie des Inscriptions et Belles-Lettres, for which Delisle was secretary, gave the priest a gold medal.

More acclaim followed, and outside Turin, the number of shroud defenders shrank appreciably.

The debate, however, wasn't yet over.

CHAPTER 2

■■■■■■■■

VIGNON AND DELAGE

nother French notable intrigued by the shroud was Yves Delage—but not for the same reason as Chevalier. Delage was a celebrated zoologist and professor of anatomy at Paris's Sorbonne. He was impressed with the photographic mystery of the shroud. An ancient linen with negative images on it? As an agnostic, Delage didn't believe in miracles. There had to be a natural explanation.

He discussed this with a young assistant, Paul Vignon, with whom he'd become close when Vignon took a staff position on Delage's popular publication, *Biology Year*. A biologist and practicing Catholic, Vignon was also, in his spare time, an amateur painter, uniquely suited to investigate the mystery. In response to Vignon's interest, Delage offered the younger scientist his lab and support to work on the problem. Vignon, who also believed there must be a natural explanation, readily accepted.

■ ■ ■ ■ ■ ■ ■ ■

Vignon may have been a Catholic, but he was determined not to let religion influence his probe. "For us," he later wrote, "the shroud is simply a large piece of linen . . . discolored by time; worn and torn in places; half burnt by fire—bearing upon its surface shadowy impressions." There would be no conclusions based on traditions or preconceived ideas, he pledged.

Acquiring shroud photos from a still-smarting and willing Pia, Vignon first tried to determine if the cloth had indeed been painted.

The artist would have had to know how to paint in reverse shading—that is, to paint the opposite of what is seen in normal light. Vignon concluded that any attempt at such a feat centuries before the concept of positive and negative images had been developed was just about inconceivable.

Even if an artist had the genius and the know-how, how could he have checked his work? And how could anyone else have been able to appreciate it? In both cases, the artist would have needed the positive and negative images photography produced. Why would he go to all the trouble to produce an image that would not be intelligible to those who saw it? And what could possibly motivate him to do a painting like this?

But there were other possibilities as well. Perhaps the negative images on the shroud were produced by some natural process following painting. Perhaps wear and tear had caused an inversion in the color of the paints over a period of time. Perhaps heat had done the trick over a short period of time.

As one critic wrote,

The flesh tints may have been painted with a mixture of white paint,which is usually an oxide of lead or of zinc combined with reds (sulphate of mercury), ochers, or naturally tinted earths;

the shadows may have been done with black paint mixed with the same ochers and natural burnt earths, or even with bitumen (petroleum). [Then] the Holy Shroud passed through critical periods, such as the fire in 1532 when the constitution of its colors must have been considerably modified . . . the [light] bitumen burnt [and] turned dark because of contamination of the atmosphere.

All such theories, however, depended on one essential fact: the presence of paint on the cloth. On examining the photographs with a magnifying glass, Vignon couldn't find a trace of paint. Moreover, when he himself painted a portrait on a piece of linen approximating the shroud material and subsequently folded it into a small square, the paint flaked off. If the shroud had been folded and unfolded, rolled and unrolled as it had for at least five centuries, painted-on images simply could not have survived.

Dyes were another possibility. But if the images were dyed onto the cloth, there wouldn't be enough consistency in them to invert into a negative image. They would have remained the same whether positive or negative. Even if there was consistency, the images, he could see, were monochromatic—the color being variously described as brown or rusty red. But the light parts of the images were from the natural color of the cloth itself—not any dye

> **Unmasking the Artist: Leonardo da Vinci?**
>
> Due to the amazing photographic quality of the shroud, some proponents of the "artist theory" have suggested that Leonardo da Vinci created the image, using a rudimentary camera that he invented. This theory has little credibility, however, especially given that the shroud first came to prominence nearly a century before Leonardo was born.

or pigment. The cloth's fibers were not an artist's creation and, anyway, had not inverted.

The images, Vignon concluded, were not painted.

Vignon's second theory involved direct contact of the cloth with the body. Wearing a fake mustache to approximate the face in the shroud, Vignon lay on a table and had two aides apply powdered chalk—red chalk, since that would show up better than white— to his face. The aides then pressed over his face a cloth resembling the shroud in texture. To everyone's surprise, when the cloth was raised, it contained a negative image of Vignon's face; the darks were light and the lights were dark. But the image itself was a disappointment. The eyes, cheeks, and mouth were too low; the nose was flattened. It was at best a caricature, and nothing at all like the precise, well-proportioned face on the linen surface of the shroud.

Twice more the scientists tried the experiment—once using less pressure than the first time, and once using more pressure. The results were the same: the chalk contacts were little more then smears.

What had happened, Vignon reasoned, had a logical explanation. "Contact alone could not render on a flat surface a true and undistorted impression of a cylindrical object," wrote John Walsh. "The flat surface would have to be wrapped around the cylinder and on being opened out again would unavoidably enlarge and distort the original object. The disparity would be more apparent where the cylinder's surface was uneven, as in a human face."

THE VAPOROGRAPH THEORY

Vignon's third theory had to do with gases and vapors rising from the body and acting chemically on the shroud in such a way as to produce the body images. He got the idea while reading of photographic film experiments being conducted by Rene Colson, a physicist at Paris's *Ecole Polytechnique*. Together they developed a series of hypotheses which they subsequently tested experimentally.

Vignon began with a metal medallion; Colson, with a sculpture of Jesus' head. They dusted the objects with zinc powder and put them in light-tight boxes. Vignon put a film plate under his medallion; Colson put a film plate over his sculpture; the one would check vapors traveling downward; the other, upward. When they developed the plates twenty-four hours later, they saw images—negative images. The medallion was a little out of focus, but the profile was indeed recognizable.

Zinc was obviously not an element in the ointments used in

Shroud Scholar: Paul Vignon

Born in 1865 in Lyon, France, Paul Vignon was an avid mountain climber, often going on dangerous excursions in the Alps. As a young man, he was also a promising biologist, but in the late 1880s he suffered a nervous breakdown. Lying in a hospital for months, he decided to take up painting. The subtleties of the art relaxed him, and he ended a year of recuperation not only as an accomplished artist, but convinced that there was a spiritual relationship between art and science. Such a viewpoint, understandably, inclined him to the shroud.

Jewish burials, but perhaps the ointments were not the image-forming agent. Perhaps urea was. Urea is found in the bladder, of course, but it is found also in sweat—morbid sweat. The sweat of a person undergoing a crisis, especially a crisis of pain, would be urea-rich. On fermenting, it would turn into carbonate of ammonia, which in turn would emit ammoniacal vapors.

But how could these vapors make an image on a linen cloth? They surmised paste of myrrh and aloes blended with olive oil—

a recipe derived from the Old Testament—was spread, not directly on Jesus' body, but on the shroud in which the body was wrapped. Aloes consist mainly of two chemical elements: aloin and aloetine, both of which oxidize and darken into a brownish color when they come into contact with alkalies like ammonia.

To test this hypothesis, Vignon and an assistant dipped a piece of linen into a mixture of oil and aloes. Then they dipped half of the cloth into ammonia water; this half oxidized, browned, and darkened immediately. When the linen was dried, the oil and aloes on the non-dipped half turned to flakes or powder which could easily be brushed off; the stain on the other half, however, was fixed, clear, and indelible, and the fabric itself had lost none of its suppleness. So far, so good.

The next step was to test the hypothesis with an object. They picked a plaster head-form, saturated it with ammonia water, and covered it with an aloes-impregnated linen cloth. The result was a brown blur on the cloth. Then the two scientists switched to a plaster cast of a hand, onto which they slipped a suede glove larded with the aloes-and-oil mixture. Slowly, carefully, they poured the ammonia water between the cast and the glove. The result on the interior of the glove, when it was slit open, was the image of a hand, not a perfect image, but one to give validity to what Vignon later labeled the "vaporograph theory." Where the cloth was in contact with the body, the chemicals made the darkest image. Where it was not, vapors rose minute distances, staining the linen more lightly the farther they traveled.

It was a rational explanation.

A NATURAL PROCESS

He was now ready for the final investigation. Had the process of the images forming on the shroud ensued naturally?

Or had it been induced by a clever forger?

The wounds, of course, appeared to be the same as Christ's in the Gospels. There were lacerations on the head as though from thorns. The man had been beaten and stabbed in the side. He had also been crucified. No other person in history is said to have been tortured and killed in that exact way. The odds against an unknown person having undergone these same tortures by chance, Vignon figured, were astronomical. Either the images really were of Jesus, or—since he'd ruled out an artist's rendering—a body had been mutilated to look like Christ's.

But then Vignon started studying the apparent blood stains with a magnifying glass. These stains were different from the images— they were positives, not reversals. They ringed the scalp, dripped down the face, and dotted and lined the chest, forearms, hands, back, and feet. Surprisingly, most showed the characteristics of authentically dried or "clotted" blood—separation of serum and darker cellular mass. This was realism unknown to a medieval artist. It convinced Vignon, a biologist, that he was looking at real blood.

But how had it gotten on the shroud in such realistic form?

If it had just been poured on the cloth, the blood would have been absorbed into the fabric, "trapped," so to speak, between the individual threads, and simply dried as a crusty, intact mass. "When we pour blood upon a...cloth," Vignon wrote, "the fiber...absorbs the liquid by capillary action so that it spreads unevenly along the threads." A good example is the way blood stains unevenly on a gauze bandage. But most of the blood stains Vignon observed on the shroud had smooth, unbroken borders. They were almost like "photographs" of blood, he wrote. The stains on the forehead and hands were good examples—perfectly formed masses surrounded by a lighter serum ooze.

There were a few stains with broken borders, like those that ran along the lower back of the man in the shroud. But as far as

Vignon could tell, most were smooth and could not have been poured onto the cloth. They must first have dried and separated on a non-absorbent surface, such as the skin of a corpse, before being transferred to the cloth.

But the theory of simple direct contact presented problems.

If the blood had already clotted and dried, how could it have transferred? It needed to be wet in order to transfer.

He decided that, given the man's torture and the amount of morbid sweat that would have been produced, if the body had been kept cool, like in a tomb, wetness might have lingered.

But even then there were problems.

How could the transfers have been executed with the perfection seen on the shroud? If the clots had been too moist, applying pressure would have squashed them. If they hadn't been moist enough, the contact wouldn't have yielded the detail seen.

Performing a test to see how contact stains might be made, Vignon wrote: "It is [only] when the [clot] is [exactly] half dissolved—neither before nor after—that a good transfer is effected. But it is very difficult to get a perfect transfer. It is either only half transferred if there is too little contact, or, if the exposure is too long, I obtain puddles and it is useless to represent them."

The clots were thus another mystery. Although with great effort Vignon could approximate them in his laboratory, he didn't see how a forger working under medieval conditions could have done so.

Other details impressed him:

The blood flows followed the natural contours of the body—for instance, the large stain on the forehead. Artists, he noted, usually depicted such flows in straight lines or stylized droplets. However, in the shroud, he noted the flow "met in its course the two wrinkles of the forehead, and has, by this slight opposition, been forced to spread itself out, forming two small horizontal pools. Thence it continued to flow, until it ended in a tear of [dried] blood close to the eyebrow."

Also surprising was the source of the forehead blood. Judging from the many lacerations covering the head, it had been caused not, it appeared, by the traditional "wreath" of thorns—almost always depicted in Christian art—but by a full "cap" of thorns, something that covered the entire upper head. Would a forger bent on enticing Christians have gone against such tradition? Wouldn't he, by doing so, have alienated the faithful he wanted to deceive?

And that wasn't the only break with tradition. Vignon noticed other pecularities:

The nail wound was in the wrist—not the hand.

Nowhere in Christian art did he know of the nails so placed. They were always in the palm. Yet, as an anatomist, Vignon knew the wrist bones provided a stronger grip for a nail than those in the hand.

The man in the shroud was nude, although the hands covered the pelvis. Christian art almost always depicted Christ in a loin cloth. This depiction surely would have caused controversy in medieval France. A forger wouldn't have chanced it.

Everywhere Vignon investigated he found similar realism. "Artists—forgers—make things easy to understand," he wrote. "On the shroud however, the truth is often hidden—revealed only by the intricacies of nature herself!"

For instance:

At first glance, the blood trails on the arms, which were folded downward, strangely appeared to have flowed up. But envisioned as the arms would have been in crucifixion—up and outstretched—the flows made perfect sense. While the arms were extended upwards, the blood, as gravity dictated, would have coursed downward and dried. When the body was removed and the arms folded inward, the blood trails would seem as if they had flowed up.

Whip marks covered the body, mostly on the dorsal image. On the surface, they appeared to be simple lashes. But under magnification, groups of each showed varying paths, as if delivered by two different floggers, alternately lashing one after the other. At the tips of each lash were small bruises or cuts. Some were dumbbell shaped. Others resembled tiny mallets. A third tip appeared to be a small hook. Checking ancient sources, Vignon found what appeared to be the whip that was used—the feared Roman "flagrum," an instrument of punishment used in Palestine at the time of Christ.

Vignon wrote:

[It] is hardly worthwhile to emphasize how very unlikely it is that any artist having to reproduce the marks of the scourging on a human body could have imagined a system of scars so complicated as that [on the shroud]. Each kind of mark would have required special attention, special invention, and we all know how difficult it is to repeat over and over again a representation which, while preserving the same general form, should show infinite variety in detail.

All such details, one way or the other, he noted, pointed to Jesus. For instance, there was a "blotch" on the right shoulder of the dorsal image, suggesting the friction of carrying timber for a cross. One cheek was swollen and bruised, recalling the account in Matthew 26:67 about Jesus being struck in the face prior to crucifixion. The swelling showed that the bruises had been inflicted before death. The chest wound,

Piercing His Heart

But one of the soldiers pierced his side with a spear, and at once there came out blood and water.

—John 19:34

visible near one of the triangular patches, showed separation of blood parts, including serum. This not only indicated the man in the shroud was dead when pierced, but made sense of the strange wording in John 19:34 that when the lance entered Jesus' chest, out came blood and "water."

The knees of the man in the shroud were cut and bruised, particularly the left one, indicating he'd fallen on it numerous times—just as the Gospels say Jesus fell on the way to Golgotha. Not only were the feet pierced as if by a nail for crucifixion—deduced from blood flows on the dorsal image—but the fact that there was only one issue of blood from the wrist visible on the shroud struck Vignon as particularly realistic. The other wrist was covered by the placement of the hands, one over the other. But since any blood issue would have come after Jesus had been taken down—and since, by then, as the Gospels say, Jesus was dead and therefore his heart had ceased pumping—there wouldn't have been much blood in the wrist area—as shown on the shroud. And any small issue from the covered wrist would logically be hidden.

Would a medieval forger have known such realistic anatomical details?

In the end, Vignon couldn't figure out how the body had exited the shroud without distorting the picture-perfect blood stains. If they'd been wet, they would have been ruined when the cloth was removed. If dry, they would have ripped the cloth.

Was this possible proof of resurrection?

Vignon couldn't say. Such a thing was beyond scientific inquiry. But he also couldn't rule it out. After all, Christian tradition said the resurrection had happened, and Vignon could not come up with another explanation. Was he to believe that a string of unfathomable coincidences had occurred and seemingly impossible tasks had been performed to create both the body images and the differently created blood images? Or was it more probable that the body that had once been in the shroud had belonged to Jesus, to whom history says the things observable in the images actually happened?

Having found a plausible answer for the images—the vapograph—Vignon couldn't help but speculate about Jesus and the resurrection. He was a practicing Christian. Whatever the truth, he'd accomplished his task. He had found a plausible explanation for how the images had been made.

■ ■ ■ ■ ■ ■ ■ ■

Yves Delage was impressed with his assistant's work. While he was dubious that something extra-natural had occurred, he was delighted with the body of evidence Vignon presented. He saw no reason why Christ could not have been a historical person, and felt his younger colleague had proved it.

"Do you remember the joy we felt," Delage later wrote to a friend, "at having at length discovered the key to the enigma?—Vignon's 'vaporograph.'" It was the "natural explanation, luminous in its simplicity, outing miracle." The blood stains could be worked on later.

Like virtually all his scientific colleagues, Delage was a rationalist, a believer in the supremacy of reason over revelation. Theirs was an era ushered in by the publication of Darwin's theory of evolution (1859), which underlined inconsistency between the Genesis account of instantaneous creation and the biological belief of man's slow emergence from lower life forms. While not an active anti-religionist, Delage would eventually receive the international "Darwin Medal" for research into the mysteries of cellular life. Vignon's work, he decided, would be an excellent presentation for his colleagues at the academy. Just the year before, Delage had been voted into the prestigious body. Explaining away this so-called "miracle" would be appreciated.

Vignon, at the time, was preparing to publish his research in a book to be titled *The Shroud of Christ*. Not a member of the academy, he was honored by Delage's proposal. Having his work singled out for such an august audience was recognition beyond anything he had imagined. Elated, he began to prepare notes from which Delage would speak.

CHAPTER 3

■■■■■■■■

A CASE OF SCIENTIFIC BIAS

In 1902, *Marcellin P. Berthelot*, often called the founder of modern organic chemistry, was one of France's most celebrated scientists—if not the world's. He was permanent secretary of the French Academy, having succeeded the giant Louis Pasteur, the renowned microbiologist. Unlike Delage, an agnostic, Berthelot was an atheist—and militantly so.

As an academy officer, Berthelot got first look at presentations to its members. He had the right to challenge. He had only to see the title of Vignon's researches to launch a formal protest. "The Shroud of Christ" is not the kind of topic to be put before the academy, he informed Delage. Delage, however, appealed the ruling and won—a reversal which surely angered the secretary.

While in college, Berthelot had met and become lifelong friends with the philosopher Ernest Renan, who, as a seminarian following a crisis of faith, had written a book challenging Christ's divinity, and gone on to become France's most towering rationalist. Spurred by Renan, Berthelot became a leading advocate for the supremacy of science over religion.

And he had impact.

Before Berthelot, it had been generally believed that the formation of organic substances required the involvement of mysterious life processes. He grandly quashed this belief with a series of experiments he conducted demonstrating that organic chemistry was dependent on the same mechanistic laws as inorganic chemistry.

Berthelot became as celebrated as Renan.

By the time he took his chair at the academy, the secretary had become France's Minister of Public Instruction, and had presided in the government which had defied Vatican wishes and secularized all the schools of France. In 1904, in a letter to a rationalist group, Berthelot would call for the eradication of "the poisonous vapours of superstition," of which Christianity, he said, was the worst. So, to his great dissatisfaction, the academy halls were filled on the day Delage was to speak.

ADDRESSING THE ACADEMY

"A crowd of well over 200 people had managed to find space in the long, rather narrow, high-ceilinged room," writes John Walsh. Among the audience of scholars, reporters, clergy, and laymen sat Paul Vignon and, in a special gallery with other academy luminaries, a reluctant Berthelot. As one reporter wrote, only once before—when Pasteur had made his dramatic report in 1885 on the rabies vaccine—had the hall been so full.

Delage, bearded and black-suited, sat attentively as those before him spoke. When finally his name was called, he went to the front, arranged Pia's photos on a blackboard, and began. In a half hour long talk, he presented the shroud's known history, explained the positive-negative enigma, detailed the extraordinary realism and unorthodoxy of the images—which he said convinced him they were not made "by the hand of man"—and offered the vaporo-graph as the scientific explanation:

> Thus M. Vignon's idea, to which I completely subscribe, is that the body... was covered with a febrile sweat rich in urea; that the urea formed ammonium carbonate which, in a calm atmos-phere, emitted vapours [sic] more and more diluted as they were farther from the emitting surface; that the shroud was soaked in an emulsion of aloes which became brown under the influ-ence of these alkaline vapours and formed a tint the more intense the nearer this surface; whence the negative image whose characteristics I described before.

About Jesus he said:

> On the one hand we have a shroud, probably impregnated with aloes—which brings us to the East outside Egypt [where mummi-fication was the rule]. And we have a crucified man who had been scourged, pierced on the right side, and crowned with thorns. On the other hand we have an account—pertaining to history, leg-end, and tradition—showing us Christ as having undergone in Judea the same treatment as we decipher on the body whose image is on the shroud. Is it not natural to bring together these two parallel series and connect them to the same object?

> Add to that the fact that, in order for the images to be "pro-duced and not later destroyed, it is necessary that the body"

remain in the shroud "at least twenty-four hours, the time [Vignon found] necessary for the formation of the image, and at most a few days, after which supervenes putrefaction which destroys the image and finally the shroud. Now this is precisely what tradition—more or less apocryphal, I admit—asserts to have happened to Christ who died on Friday and disappeared on Sunday."

So here was "a collection of five circumstances, to mention only the principal, which are rather exceptional: the East outside Egypt, the wound in the side, the crown of thorns, the duration of the burial, the character of the physiognomy. Suppose that for each there should be one chance in a hundred that it should occur in the case of another person. There would then be only one chance in ten thousand million that they should be found together." Delage admitted that his math might not be exact. "But those who wish to attribute the shroud to another person are in the same condition as ourselves with respect to the other difficulties, with this difference—that their person is a pure invention without any mention in history, tradition or legend."

Pope Pius VII and the Shroud

Pope Pius VII (1800-1823) presided over two expositions of the shroud. The first was in Turin on November 13, 1804, as the pope made his way to France to crown Napoleon emperor. (Napoleon insisted he must be crowned by the pope himself, and forced the pope to come from Italy to preside over the coronation ceremony. For the pope's pains, Napoleon had him imprisoned, making him a captive of the Napoleonic Empire.) The second exposition took place in 1815, on the pope's return to Italy from France, after Napoleon's defeat. Standing on the balcony of the Palazzo Madama, the Holy Father himself held the shroud up for the crowd below to see.

BIAS WINS OUT

Press reports show Delage's speech caused a sensation. "Photographs of Christ's Body Found by Science," blared a headline in the Paris edition of the *New York Herald* (April 22, 1902). "It may be said without hesitation that [Vignon and Delage] raised a question of the most absorbing interest," echoed the *London* and *New York Times*. *The Lancet*, a highly-respected British medical journal, reported (April 26) that "M. Vignon's paper has created an extreme interest both in the scientific and the religious world."

But the praise, as with Pia's photographs, was short lived. As later reported by Arthur Loth, an academy history laureate present at Delage's speech, Berthelot—as was his right—had refused to allow a customary vote of confidence to be taken by the academy after Delage's presentation. As Delage spoke, explained Loth in a book he later wrote, the secretary had "pretended not to hear and affected to write all the time." Further, Berthelot censored Delage's presentation paper later published in the academy's journal, *Comptes Rendus*. All mentions of Christ—central to the vaporograph—had been expunged.

In addition, Father Ulysee Chevalier, feeling challenged by Vignon and Delage, had entered the public discussion. The relic lacks a documented beginning, he reminded in a series of articles, and, most importantly, the D'Arcis Memorandum proves the shroud a fake. He erroneously reported that the full academy had refused "to ratify the communication of M. Delage" when, in fact, only Berthelot had prevented it. But few outside the academy were aware of the error. The press turned on Delage. Outraged at this turn of events, historian Loth wrote, "The statement of M. Chevalier... is absolutely incorrect." Chevalier "was not at the [meeting and] it is very probable [the academy] would have been unanimous in adopting the scientific point of view of the report, and in admitting the impression on the shroud could not, in any way, have been a painting."

But as in 1898, the defense came too late. Chevalier's articles renewed suspicion of Pia. The old charges of photo manipulation again flew. The Church, burnt so often by spurious relics, sided with Chevalier. The Jesuit-dominated periodical *Analecta Bollandiana*, for instance, declared Chevalier's arguments "final." Protestants just shrugged. For them, the relic was "too Catholic." The Vatican remained aloof, although Chevalier erroneously said they agreed it was a fake. Vignon, a mere young assistant, was powerless. He didn't have stature. Delage, at first feisty, retreated and became embittered. Writing an open letter to a friend, the editor of Paris's *Review Scientific*, Delage confided:

> When some months ago I went to see you in your laboratory to introduce to you M. Vignon . . . did you anticipate the passionate disputes which would be excited in the press. . . . No; you did not . . . naively we thought it was believers—at least those whose minds were enslaved by a too narrow religion—who would be in opposition to us. . . .

But it was scientific bias, he felt, that had ultimately done them in. "If [Vignon's researches] have not received from certain people the welcome they deserved, the sole reason is that there has been unfairly grafted on to this scientific question a religious issue which has excited men's minds and misled right reason." If it hadn't been Jesus in question, but someone like "Sargon or Achilles or one of the Pharaohs," Delage asserted, "there would have been no objection."

He continued:

In refusing to insert my note in the proceedings, it has been for-gotten that this publication [*Comptes Rendus*] contains matters which are much more hypothetical—theories . . . corroborated by no experiment, and many others based upon arguments far more fragile than those brought forward here. But then there was no question of matters touching religion. There lies all the difference.

He had been "faithful to the scientific spirit," he concluded. "I consider Christ a historical person, and I see no reason why peo-ple should be scandalized if there exists a material trace of his exis-tence. As to the question of [His divinity], I have said nothing, because I have nothing to say."

■■■■■■■■

By this time the shroud itself had long since been put away. Shortly after Pia's photos were taken, a procession of mitered and chanting bishops had entered into the chapel's cavernous confines, paused in front of its towering black and gold altar, and after cer-emoniously opening three separate locks, deposited the linen in its rectangular silver coffin with a symbolically permanent clang.

It would not be exhibited again until 1931.

PART II
1973

·········

A REPORTER'S
SEARCH

CHAPTER 4

■■■■■■■■

AN EXPOSITION

MIAMI

● ● ● ● ● ● ● ● ●

"*They're going to show the shroud after* all these years? You've got to be kidding!" I didn't mean to be rude, especially when the other party was calling me long distance (very expensive in 1973). But the shroud hadn't been shown publicly for forty years (not since 1933), and only twice before that in the last 100 years—in 1931 and in 1898.

"I've just returned from Turin. There really is going to be a public exposition, this time on television.... "

The voice on the other end of the line was shaky, not only because Father Peter Rinaldi had recently had a throat operation, but because he could hardly contain his enthusiasm.

"And the cardinal has assured me that all experts invited to Turin for the occasion will see the shroud in person."

Rinaldi, who had been an interpreter for non-Italian-speaking visitors to the 1933 exposition, was one of America's leading sindonologists. A Salesian priest in Port Chester, New York, in the 1970s, he had been prodding the Turin authorities for the previous nine years to show the shroud in public again. His hope, along with that of the other sindonologists around the world, was that such an exposition would lead to a full-scale scientific investigation, which, in turn, would lead to a final vindication of the shroud as the linen cloth put around the body of Jesus after it was taken down from the cross.

"When is the exposition going to take place?" I asked.

"In about three months' time—around Thanksgiving."

"Can you get me a pass to attend as one of the experts?"

I wasn't really an expert, but I had been writing about the shroud for more than two years. My interest in it had been aroused by a wire story I'd read about a German who believed that Christ had not died on the cross. What impressed me about the shroud was not so much the arguments deduced from it— although they were impressive—but the fact that something else besides the New Testament might exist as proof that Jesus Christ really had lived. I had made a quick trip to Turin, visited the Center for Sindonology there, interviewed as many sindonologists as I could find in that city and in Rome, then returned home to Miami to write four articles on the shroud. They appeared first on the front pages of the newspaper I worked for, the *Miami News,* and later in syndication through the North American Newspaper Alliance, Christmas 1971. Here was a chance to learn more.

"That shouldn't be a problem," said the priest. "Just send me a letter saying you'll be covering the event for your newspaper."

NEW SHROUD PHOTOS

Before leaving Miami, I stuffed my briefcase full of the clippings, articles, and books about the shroud that I had amassed over the past two years. There would be many moments to fill during my trip, and if I wanted to write again about the shroud, this time in depth, I would have to master every detail of its history and every theory about its origin.

The first thing I picked out of my case was a batch of clippings having to do with the world reaction to the Pia photographs. They had caused quite a sensation. But after the initial reaction, the shroud, attacked for various reasons, had been forgotten except in isolated places, like Turin, and later (after its establishment in 1950) Father Rinaldi's church in Port Chester, New York. Not until May 3, 1931, the first day of a 21-day exposition during which two million people would pass by the shroud in Turin's St. John's Cathedral, would the shroud catapult back into prominence.

What brought the shroud back to prominence were new photographs—the first taken of the shroud since those made by Pia in 1898. What happened was this: After the great doors of St. John's were shut at 10:30 p.m. on the night of May 3, 1931, Giuseppe Enrie, a new figure in the shroud story, walked down the center aisle toward the main altar just as Pia had decades before. Enrie, editor of *Vita Photographica Italiana* and owner of a photo studio and laboratory in Turin, had been asked to take new photos of the shroud, not only to put together a more professional set than Pia had made a generation before, but also to verify—or negate—what Pia claimed to have found on his negative plates.

As it had been for Pia, the pressure was on.

The shroud was exhibited high and hanging in a gilded frame over the main altar. The first step in the photographing process was to take it down from its lofty perch. Maurilio Cardinal Fossati, archbishop of Turin, directed the move, and several prelates mounted the tiered altar and unscrewed the bolts that held the 15-foot frame in place. Slowly, carefully, they handed the frame to priests waiting below, who then placed it at the foot of the altar. This took about fifteen minutes.

Noticing that areas in the cloth, especially around the top of the head and the lower chin, marred the image, Fossati unfastened the linen from the frame, smoothed it out, and refastened it. The creases were still visible. Father Antonio Tonelli, an expert in the textile aspects of the shroud, tried his hand at smoothing the creases, but he also had no success. By now, fifteen more minutes had passed, and Enrie, who had already set up the lights and camera, was getting impatient. With a shrug, Fosatti motioned to the photographer to begin.

Enrie focused first on the burn patches; they were the easiest marks to see. He checked the image in the viewfinder with a magnifying glass. Then he opened the shutter for a time exposure. When nine minutes had passed, he closed the shutter, took the photographic plate out of the camera, and rushed toward the sacristy where he had set up a makeshift darkroom.

With the help of Secondo Pia, now seventy-six years old, and two others, Enrie set about developing the plate. One hundred sixty seconds passed, so the story goes, before Pia shouted, "It's the same!" There in the tray of chemicals was the face he knew so well—only this time the image was clearer and sharper. Enrie took the plate out of the developer and held it up to the light. There was no question about it—the revelation had been repeated! They hurried back to the sanctuary to show the plate to the cardinal and his staff.

By 12:30 a.m., Enrie exposed six more plates, each focused on the shroud as a whole. He and his friends spent the rest of the night developing the plates, and by 10:00 a.m. they were ready to submit the resulting prints to the cardinal for his inspection. Six days later the prints were stamped "Authorized for reproduction," and copies were sent to a number of publications around the world.

On May 19, Enrie took three more photographs of the shroud, which was still on display in its glass-covered frame; each shot was of one-third of the cloth; the result was a composite of the whole shroud, and these, too, were officially approved.

On the evening of May 22, Enrie took three close-ups of the shroud without its glass covering: one of the face, one of the back and shoulders, and, with a lens that would magnify seven times, one of the wound on the wrist.

To avoid the same kind of charges of fraud that had plagued Pia after his 1898 photographs had been distributed around the world, Enrie invited five professional photographers to study his plates. They verified that none had been retouched, and that all had accurately captured what the naked eye could see on the surface of the shroud. They signed a document swearing to these conclusions.

From that time on, Pia's photographs were retired, and the Enrie photographs became the official pictures of the shroud given out by ecclesiastical authorities in Turin. The charges of hanky-panky in the darkroom have never been brought up again.

A DOCTOR AT CALVARY

Among those who benefited from the new Enrie photos was French physician Pierre Barbet, who would become president of Paris's Society of Surgeons. I had his 1953 book, *Doctor at Calvary*. A friend who had attended the exposition brought him life-size blowups of the new photographs. The friend wanted to know what he thought of the body images in the shroud. Studying them, Barbet was impressed with the anatomical realism.

As head surgeon of St. Joseph's Hospital, Paris, Barbet had access to unclaimed bodies and body parts from operations. With a freshly amputated arm, he decided to test the unusual placing of the nails through the wrists, as shown on the shroud image. He could see the nails had been driven into the arm in an area called "Destot's Space," a circular indenture in the middle of the wrist. He also knew that the wrist was a tight assemblage of seven small bones called carpals, interlocked with ligaments. He thought a nail there would injure the carpals. To his surprise, though, as he drove a large nail through them, they parted, allowing the nail to pass through. Once the nail was in place, the carpals clamped tightly around it. More surprising was the fact that, in the instant the nail had been hammered, the thumb snapped into the palm.

At first Barbet was baffled. But then he realized the nail had hit a nerve, which would cause this reaction. This coincided exactly with the thumbless hands on the shroud, a curiosity that he now realized was a starkly realistic detail. "Is it possible that trained executioners wouldn't have known about this ideal spot for crucifying hands," he later wrote—but that a forger would have? It was impressive realism.

But would the nail hold the weight of a crucified body?

The only way to find out, of course, would be to crucify a body himself. And that is precisely what Barbet did—with one of the cadavers to which he had access. He placed a cross flush on the floor, with the upright about seven feet in length, and the crossbar intersecting it about one foot from the top of the upright. He rolled the corpse onto the cross and stretched its arms out at right angles. Poising a square nail—the sort of nail the Romans used—in Destot's space, he drove it through the flesh and into the wood with one blow; then he nailed the other hand. He next drove a nail through the middle of the left foot; then, pressing the sole of the right foot flush against the wood, he drove the same nail through the flesh and into the cross.

Raising the cross from the floor, Barbet knew that his theories would literally either stand or fall when he and his aides brought the cross to a totally upright position and slid the beam into a hole on the platform. When they did so, the body slumped down about ten inches. The chest area expanded in size as though the victim had taken a deep breath and was about to exhale. The head was pulled forward and down, with the chin touching the collarbone. The knees jutted out. The body stayed on the cross.

AN AUDIENCE WITH THE KING

My first stop in Europe was Lisbon, Portugal, where I planned to meet with Umberto of Savoy, Italy's exiled monarch. Umberto, who was crown prince of Italy in 1931 prior to World War II, and the last king of that country before the abolition of his rule in a 1946 post-war plebiscite called to punish the Savoys for Italy's ties to the Axis, lived in Portugal, near Lisbon. Since he and his family had owned the shroud for centuries, it was logical to assume that he would most certainly know more about it than anyone else. As I drove from the airport in Lisbon north along the road to the Savoy villa in Cascais—Father Rinaldi had arranged the interview—I hoped the king would be able to tell me who actually controlled the shroud.

In fifty miles' time, I reached the small, picturesque fishing village with its masted boats bobbing all around the circumference of the blue bay. Crossing a bridge at the northern tip of the bay, I found the king's mansion overlooking the Atlantic. "Villa Italia" read the inscription on the stone wall. The iron gates were open, and I drove up a short, pebbled driveway to a large, two-story

stone house. A servant opened the heavy wooden doors and ushered me into a drawing room, the first room to the left off a short,
high-ceilinged entrance hall. In a moment the king's secretary
appeared, and, after conferring with someone behind him hidden
from my view, escorted me inside.

The king lifted his hand in greeting. "How is Father Rinaldi?"
he asked me in English. He appeared taller than he did in pictures
I'd seen of him standing beside his father, and younger than his
seventy years.

The room was a large study lined with portraits of Savoys. Papers
lay strewn over a massive desk. The king was in the midst of writing his memoirs, or so he said. We sat down. As I began to set up
the tape recorder, he put up his hand. He was sorry, but he could
not allow the interview to be recorded. I'd have to take notes.

The talk began with the king describing some scenes of the various expositions he'd attended and knew something about.

Prior to the 1898 exposition, he said, Princess Clotilde
(1843–1911) got down on her knees and mended the deteriorated
backing of the shroud. This was an indication of how revered the
shroud was among his family members.

At the time of the 1933 exposition, a *New York Times* report
had said there was an old belief within the royal house that as
long as the shroud remained in the possession of the Savoys, the
house would never fall; yet the house had fallen after the 1946
plebiscite which established a republic in Italy, replacing the historical monarchy. I mentioned this story to the king; he said he
was not familiar with the belief.

The shroud was shown only on important occasions, mostly
family ones. The 1898 exposition had been held in honor of the
wedding of his father, Victor Emmanuel III; and of course the
1931 exposition had commemorated his own wedding. The 1933
exposition had been held in honor of the 1900th anniversary of

Christ's death and resurrection. To show the shroud more often, he said, would make it commonplace.

"Who controls the shroud?" I asked.

"Before I left Turin," the king replied, "the family always made decisions concerning the shroud—after consultation with the pope, of course. During World War II, my father ordered that the shroud be taken to southern Italy because of the possibility that it might be damaged by bombs. When the war ended, I personally ordered it back to Turin. But when I left Italy, I told the archbishop of Turin that he would be in charge. 'I won't be here,' I said, 'so you will know best what to do.' That is the way it has remained. He makes the final decisions."

The king said he would favor scientific tests on the shroud, but the initiative would have to come from Turin. There was a security problem right now, he went on; twice in recent months attempts had been made to steal the shroud from the chapel in which it resides. No one had been caught, and the chapel was now rigged with an elaborate alarm system.

A Royal Gift

When King Umberto II of Savoy died in 1983, he transferred ownership of the shroud, in his family's hands for centuries, to the Catholic Church.

Half an hour had passed, and voices could be heard in the drawing room. "I am sorry," the king's secretary said, "but others are waiting." The king rose, I thanked him, and as I left the room, four well-dressed men entered, kissed the king's hand, and said that they wished he still were king.

As I pulled out of the driveway and headed back to Lisbon airport, the king was on the front steps of his villa posing for pictures.

CHAPTER 5

■■■■■■■■

SECRET COMMISSIONS, EVASIVE RESPONSES

A COLD RECEPTION IN ITALY

S *now was on the Alps when I arrived in Turin*, and after I had warmed up, I decided to go to the archdiocesan office. I wanted to interview Fossati's successor, Michele Cardinal Pellegrino, and pick up whatever material about the shroud the office might have prepared for foreign journalists who no doubt would be covering the event.

What I noticed initially upon entering the building was the lack of activity. The first showing of the shroud in forty years was surely a historic occasion, and I had expected it to generate high, if subdued, excitement. I later found out that once the archdiocese had decided to announce the exposition, it had launched what it felt was an elaborate campaign to publicize the event: special commissions were appointed, proclamations issued, newspaper articles written, Eucharists celebrated, and a security firm hired. But that was a month ago. Now, a few days before the event, none of this material was available in the Turin chancery.

Suddenly I was confronted with a problem. I didn't speak Italian, no one in the chancery spoke English, and what little printed matter I could pick up was not in English.

When I returned later with an interpreter from the hotel, I got little more information. There would be a press conference on Friday in preparation for the exposition on Saturday. I might be able to get an interview with the cardinal later in the week. Only the cardinal and his spokesman, Monsignor José Cottino, knew the details, and they were not available for interview right now.

My interpreter was an elderly woman who was accustomed to dealing with tourists. As a go-between to extract information, she was less than adequate, for when given vague replies, or no answer at all, she did not press for more. I decided to return to my hotel, the Ambasciatori, to get a new translator.

INTERVIEWING MONSIGNOR COTTINO

Monsignor Cottino finally agreed to speak with me. It had taken a lot of asking on my part, and I think he was tired of my requests. When the appointed time arrived, he came quickly into the small room adjoining the shroud chapel where I and my new translator, a more able woman than the first, were waiting early Tuesday morning. He looked harried and announced with half a smile that he didn't have much time; he asked me to be brief.

I decided to skip preliminaries and get right to the point.

Direct Contact: A Failed Hypothesis

In 1939 a sindonological congress was held in Turin. One of the topics under discussion was the burial of Jesus. Was he buried hastily, or was his body given a full ritual interment? If the body had not been washed, then the images on the shroud could have been formed by vapors rising from the sweat, as Paul Vignon theorized. But if the body had been not only washed, but also packed with spices, then the images on the shroud could have been formed by direct contact, or so the theory went.

Prior to the congress, two Italian pathologists had conducted experiments by spreading aloes, myrrh, turpentine, olive oil, and sometimes animal blood on the faces of corpses available to them. They then applied linen cloths to the contours of the faces in an attempt to lift off an image as sharp as the shroud's.

"Prof. Romanese of the Royal University of Turin and Prof. Judica-Cordiglia of the Royal University of Milan have presented extraordinary results," wrote Turin's newspaper *L'Italia*. "They have made imprints that even have the diffusion of the shroud without, of course, surpassing its beauty or perfection. This encourages the possibility of some day being able to make imprints exactly like the shroud's."

When the official record of the 1939 proceedings was published in 1941, it referred to Romanese and Judica-Cordiglia as pioneers. In reality, however, the contact images they produced fell far short of the realism exhibited by the shroud itself. Not only did the faces appear smudged and unreal, but they did not show the tiny recesses of the body, like the sides of the nose, things that would not come into direct contact with a burial cloth. This attempt, like all others so far, failed to reproduce images like those on the shroud.

I was interested in a nearly secret investigation conducted on the shroud in 1969. It had been held between June 16 and 18 of that year. It was extraordinary in that few if any had seen the relic since 1933, and it was unpublicized, which gave it an air of mystery. What had finally been briefly announced was that Cardinal Fossati and his successor, Cardinal Pellegrino, had assembled a commission of experts to examine what, if any, hurtful effects mounting industrial pollution in Turin might be having on the shroud; also, it was said, they were determining if tests like Carbon 14 dating could be performed without detriment to the shroud. When the authorities were finally forced to admit such a study took place, they refused to name the commission members or to release their findings.

"What were the findings of the secret 1969 commission?" I asked.

"There have been no results beyond what was announced in early 1970," he answered. "We have told the press that many times. The commission members were only to see what condition the relic was in. And the only thing that could be determined on the spot was that the man in charge of deciding if the Carbon 14 test could be used decided that it could not be."

"Why?"

"Carbon 14 would damage the shroud," Cottino replied. "The test involves burning a piece of the material, and too large a piece would have to be destroyed. And there is no assurance that the test would be accurate. Carbon 14 can only give you a date accurate within two hundred years, plus or minus. And the cloth had been handled so much, and been in and out of at least two fires. Its carbon content might very well have been affected under such adverse conditions. Carbon 14 is good for objects that have been protected in the earth or in caves, but not for the shroud."

I pressed further.

"Are you sure nothing else resulted from the commission members examining the shroud for three days?"

"Yes, I'm sure. There was nothing else," he said. "You must understand I can only answer your religious questions pertaining to the shroud. The cardinal is the only one who can tell you anything about the commission."

"But aren't you one of the commission officers?"

"Please, I can tell you nothing more about the commission. If you have something to ask me about the exposition, perhaps I can help."

"How about the names of the commission members?"

Cottino's half smile turned to a look of irritation. "We feel that the commission members will be better able to complete their work if they are not known," he said. "We do not want a great debate going on while they are working."

My translator was becoming embarrassed by the tone of the exchange. I decided to change the subject to the exposition.

Here Cottino opened up a bit. He explained that the idea behind this upcoming exposition was to increase devotion to the shroud by showing it to as many people as possible. By putting it on Italian television, the exposition would reach millions of Italians, and the authorities would be able to gauge their devotional as well as political reactions. "The shroud was always a symbol of the monarchy," he said, "especially right after the war."

When I asked a question about the history of the shroud, Cottino referred me to Father Piero Coero-Borga, author of *The Holy Shroud of Turin*, which was published in 1961 by the Confraternity of the Shroud in Turin, and secretary of the Center of Sindonology, the shroud museum in Turin.

FATHER COERO-BORGA FILLS ME IN

When Father Piero Coero-Borga greeted me at the door of the shroud museum, he was unpretentious, almost businesslike. Like Cottino, he didn't have much time to discuss the shroud; he was heavily involved, he said, in preparations for the exposition. But he did take the time to show me and my interpreter around the museum, which was one building of several surrounding a small, paved square that was open to the sky. The museum wasn't very big—nothing more than a large room really—with items from the shroud's past on shelves and tables. Secondo Pia's camera was the biggest display piece; it stood in one corner, like a finely carpentered, natural-grained doghouse on stilts. Positioned carefully on a table in the center of the room were books of clippings going back to 1900. A gallery of shroud personalities—mostly Italian—glowered from the walls.

When the tour was over, the three of us walked across the courtyard to Coero's office. Letters from shroud enthusiasts all over the world were stacked on his desk, and as curator of the museum and custodian of all official shroud information, he would answer them all. After we sat down, I brought up the secret commission again, asking him who the members were.

"I would like to tell you," Coero replied, "but we were all sworn to secrecy. If, however, you read the newspapers, you may learn something."

From a desk drawer he pulled out a handful of clippings, handed them to me, and then turned to his voluminous correspondence. While he was thus engaged, I went through the clippings with my translator. I checked for outright admissions, for facts that only commission members would know, for details about the photographing of the shroud that had not been released by the archdiocese. With the aid of these and other sources, I was able to piece together a list of probable commission members; some of the names I would eventually verify, while others would remain simply good guesses.

The commission probably had eleven members. Three were clerics involved in one way or another with the shroud: Cardinal Pellegrino, Monsignor Cottino, and Monsignor Pietro Caramello, rector of St. John's Cathedral. The eight others were scientists of one sort or another. Giovanni Judica-Cordiglia's specialty was forensic medicine, which he taught and practiced in Milan. He had participated in earlier shroud congresses, including the one in 1939. Giovanni Frache taught pathology at the University of Modena; Cesare Codegone and Enzo Delorenzi were radiologists. E. Medi was a physicist from the University of Rome. Anthropologist Luigi Gedda also participated in the 1939 congress, and took some measurements of the shroud in 1946 when it was being shown to the monks at Monte Vergine, where the shroud was taken for safekeeping during World War II.

In addition to the Italians, there was a Swiss police pathologist, Max Frei, who had assisted in the investigation of United Nations General Secretary Dag Hammarskjold's death in 1961. An evangelical Protestant, Frei was the only non-Catholic on the commission. He would later date the shroud with pollens.

The only non-cleric and nonscientist who might have been on the commission was Lorenzi Ferri, a sculptor involved in size-of-Christ debates in the early 1950s.

"The commission found nothing new, you know," said Coero, pausing from his correspondence. "For them everything has already been decided. They are living in the past. They think the 1930s were the glory years and nothing new can be found. For me, it is impossible to think that anyone could examine the shroud in 1969 and not find something new."

"The archdiocese," he added, "was ready to let some of the scientists of the commission take out a small part of the shroud with blood on it. But the scientists could not get together on how to examine it. When the authorities saw the disagreement, they decided such liberty would not be wise."

It was noon. I thanked Coero and, with my interpreter, headed for the door. But before we reached it, he advised me to check the guest list at the Ambasciatori. Perhaps some of the commission members would be coming to Turin for the exposition.

As I left, I felt that the shroud was doomed to be forever enveloped in official secrecy. Perhaps I could get a few rays of light from the cardinal, with whom I had an appointment in the afternoon.

The Shroud Escapes the Nazis

During World War II, the Nazis made repeated requests to see the shroud, allegedly for scholarly and devotional purposes. Cardinal Fossati didn't trust them, however, and avoided giving them direct answers. He'd already spirited the shroud to a stone fortress overlooking Avellino, 140 miles south of Rome. Built in the twelfth century and accessible only by a dirt road, the building now was the Benedictine monastery of Monte Vergine. When the shroud arrived, it was placed in a wooden box, sealed, and hidden under the main altar in the chapel. If the monastery were bombed, the monks could rush it to a cave in the heart of the mountain.

1950: THE FIRST INTERNATIONAL SHROUD CONGRESS

Before 1969, the last official congress on the shroud had been held in 1950. Unlike the 1969 commission, this congress was known to the public, and its proceedings given full coverage by the press. On May 1, 1950, the first international shroud congress was convened in the Majestic Pontifical Chancellery Palace near the Vatican in Rome. The Turin *cultores*, hosts of the congress, had invited scholars from all over the world to come to the eternal city and to start anew what had almost been lost in the holocaust.

Representing the United States was Father Edward Wuenschel, a professor of dogmatic theology at Mount Saint Alphonsus Redemptorist Seminary in Esopus, New York. In 1937, after considerable correspondence, Father Wuenschel had persuaded *Scientific American*, no friend of religion, to publish a shroud article by Paul Vignon, which Wuenschel had translated. In a paper entitled "The Holy Shroud and the Burial of Christ," he told the congress that the shroud was not in conflict with either the known methods of Jewish burial or New Testament Scriptures.

Representing France was Pierre Barbet, who delivered a paper, "Proof of the Authenticity of the Shroud in the Deposits of Blood," which he based on the realism exhibited by the mysterious blood images.

Also from France was Monsignor Joseph R. deMelin, vicar general of the diocese of Troyes, where in the fourteenth century Geoffrey deCharnay, church officials at Lirey, and Pierre d'Arcis had been embroiled with the shroud.

There were four delegates from Italy:

Pathologist Judica-Cordiglia delivered two papers—one on new studies of the origin of the imprints; the other on anthropological observations.

Father Pietro Scotti, professor of chemistry at the University of Genoa, gave a general overview of scientific research since 1898.

Monsignor Pietro Savio, a Vatican archivist, detailed his extensive research in the Church's libraries, searching for documents that might shed light on the misty history of the shroud.

Lorenzo Ferri, a professor at the University of Rome and a sculptor who had made a marble statue modeled on the figure in the shroud, shared his anatomical observations with the congress.

From Spain had come Dr. Tomas L. Luna of the University of Saragossa. He presented a brief history of Spain's devotion to the relic: in 1454, it seems, the kingdom of Aragon had been granted a license to collect money for the shroud; a convent in Toledo had a painting of the shroud on one of its walls; a church in Madrid had a copy of the shroud that was said to have been pressed against the shroud of Turin on May 3, 1620.

The sole German present was Dr. Hermann Moedder, a radiologist from Cologne. He reported on experiments in which he had student volunteers hang from crosses in simulated crucifixion. Unlike Barbet, Moedder believed that death was caused by the pooling of blood in the body's lower parts.

Several papers were received and read *in absentia*.

R. W. Hynek, a physician who conducted studies on the death of Christ, was to have come from Czechoslovakia to speak on the physical agonies of the crucifixion. The Communist government, however, had refused to give him a visa.

Dr. Muitz Eskenazi from Istanbul, Turkey, sent a paper attacking the authenticity of the shroud, and it was read into the record of the congress. He offered no new evidence for his position, and the arguments he used had already been refuted many times by the European and American sindonologists.

The four-day congress ended with solemn devotions in Turin, and although nothing really new came out of it, the press saw fit to give the proceedings full coverage.

DEBATES IN THE PRESS

In reporting on the 1950 congress, the secular press focused in particular on the "how-did-Christ-die" debate. The physicians at the congress had been split between asphyxiation and the pooling of blood in the body's lower parts.

The religious press, however, zeroed in on the issue of authenticity.

The first story filed by Father Max Jordan, who was covering the congress for the National Catholic News Service, dealt with the German scholars. Although not present at the meetings, they had attacked the authenticity of the shroud on scriptural grounds. Jordan's final dispatch at the end of the congress reported that evidence for and against authenticity was about even.

Somewhat later, the London *Tablet* ran a story to the effect that the impression made just by the photographs of the shroud was a very deep one. "The first thought likely to occur is: 'But how very strongly the figure resembles the Christ of any number of old masters!'"

The article concluded with a double negative: "No one who believes in the genuineness of the Holy Shroud can be accused of undue credulity."

■■■■■■■■

Another area the secular press focused on was Jesus' actual size. "How big was Jesus Christ?" asked *Time* magazine in its May 15, 1950, issue, which focused on the 1950 shroud congress. "Was be a strongly built man, 5 feet 10 inches tall, with long, delicate hands and feet, a right shoulder slightly lower than the left? Did he have a brain weighing approximately 1,492 grams?"

Lorenzo Ferri, the professor and sculptor from the University of Rome, believed that Jesus was taller than previously reported. The shroud showed him to have been 6 feet 1 or 2 inches tall, and to have had the lithe limbs of an artist. When laid in the tomb, the body was hunched up in the shape of an S, with knees bent upward and back and the neck curling forward. Therefore, when and if stretched flat, the body would be longer than the imprints on the shroud show.

Ferri was backed up in this belief by Dr. Luigi Gedda, a Roman anatomist, who said the man in the shroud was at least six feet tall. As proof, he offered measurements he had taken when the shroud was shown to the Benedictines at Monte Vergine in 1946.

Gedda also pointed out that the man in the shroud had an appreciable slump in his right shoulder and concluded that Jesus must have been a right-handed carpenter.

The *Time* story ended with an equal list of pros and cons on the authenticity of the shroud.

Other news sources also honed in on the issue of Christ's size. "How big was Jesus?" *Newsweek* asked in the lead paragraph of a story in its April 29, 1968, issue. "Pious pictures of Jesus as a tall man are not accurate. Or so claims an Italian scholar who estimates that he was a shade under 5 feet 4 inches and probably weighed about 155 pounds—a normal stature for a Palestinian of Christ's era."

The article featured Monsignor Giulio Ricci, archivist at the Vatican's Congregation for Bishops and student of the shroud for many years. Ricci had made minute calculations from the shroud photos, two huge blowups which were permanent fixtures on the walls of his spacious Rome apartment.

Ricci's first book, *The Man in the Shroud*, had been published in the 1950s. Now his later studies had interested the Vatican so much, said the *Newsweek* article, that it had published a long story on them in *L'Osservatore Della Domenica*.

Ricci based his calculations on anatomical measurements of the limbs in the shroud images. For instance, the forearms were almost 14 inches long, he said, and such a length corresponds to a 5'3" body. Previous calculations as to the height of Christ were erroneous, Ricci claimed, because they were based on measurements taken from the top of the head to the tip of the toes. The toes were extended when Christ had been placed in the shroud, and therefore, according to Ricci, measurements from or to them would make Jesus seem taller. Accurate measurements could only be made, he said, by measuring from the heel.

"Together with Dr. Nicolo Miani, professor of anatomy at Rome's Sacred Heart Medical School," continued the *Newsweek* story, "Ricci spent months wrapping corpses in winding sheets to check his calculations." He also deduced that Jesus, when whipped, had been bent over in a position similar to a man in the middle of a toe-touching exercise—probably because he had had his hands tied to a "low pillar." There were at least 98 lashes to be counted on the shroud body and perhaps as many as 120, the article quoted Ricci saying.

The *Catholic Herald*, a leading Catholic weekly in England, used the *L'Osservatore* article as the basis for a feature on Ricci at approximately the same time. And shortly thereafter *Paris-Match*, one of France's largest picture magazines, also carried a story on him, which included paintings Ricci had done on the passion of Christ as deduced from the details on the shroud.

MEETING THE CARDINAL

The cardinal's office was large and cold; the walls were built of gray stone blocks. Velvet drapes flanked the windows, dark portraits hung on the walls, and the chairs my interpreter and I sat on were upholstered in leather. On the coffee table was a copy of Rinaldi's book, *It Is the Lord*, which, I discovered on opening, was personally inscribed by the author. We sat down on the lumpy leather chairs, waiting and occasionally whispering.

Nearly an hour had passed since the time the interview with Michele Cardinal Pellegrino was supposed to have begun, when a pale-faced young man in a cassock entered the room. He motioned for us to follow him. Beyond the curtains through which he led us were a succession of rooms, and in the last of these was the cardinal. He was sitting at a desk with another curtain behind it. I put out my hand, he put out his, and we shook limply.

Before I could ask my first question, he said he wanted it understood that "all authority and answering power" had been transferred to Monsignor Cottino.

Now that was convenient. Cottino had said the same about the Cardinal.

But what could I do?

I acknowledged his statement, but before I could ask my second question, he said that a press conference would be held the next day, during the course of which all questions pertaining to the shroud exposition on television on Saturday night would be answered.

I said I knew that and was just about to ask him for a comment on the international interest in the shroud, when he said that the holy relic had inspired much devotion among the faithful.

There was nothing left to say, it seemed, but to thank him and leave.

In the cab heading back to the Ambasciatori, I concluded that the twentieth century was not a good one for public relations in Turin.

■■■■■■■■

The press conference for the Friday exposition was to be held in one of the large conference rooms of the Royal Palace. Once the former residence of the Savoys, the building had been converted into a museum, with some rooms used as city and church offices. The palace was attached to St. John's Cathedral; it also surrounded a courtyard, which was the size of a football field, in which the lavish processions of previous shroud exhibitions had taken place.

The conference was supposed to begin at 11:00 a.m., but by noon nothing had happened. Seventy-five local and foreign newsmen were supposed to be in the room, as well as a number of shroud experts from around the world, but far fewer than that seemed to be in attendance.

While waiting, I struck up a conversation with a young woman. Pretty and blond, she was from *Newsweek*'s Rome bureau. She too had learned of the exposition through Rinaldi, and she had interviewed a shroud expert in Rome before coming to Turin. She spoke Italian.

CHAPTER 6

■■■■■■■■

SEEING THE SHROUD

A CARDINAL'S ADDRESS

• •

A**t 1:00 p.m., the authorities entered** the room. Giovanni Judica-Cordiglia, the Milan pathologist, came in first; that he was one of the few shroud experts still around from the 1930s made him a celebrity. A small, thin man with skin stretched tightly across his face, and a large set of teeth, he smiled as he moved to the back of the room. A few minutes later, Monsignor Cottino and Cardinal Pellegrino arrived and went directly to the rostrum, where Cottino seated Pellegrino at a table with a microphone.

"The shroud," the cardinal began, "is a moving document of the passion of Christ."

I hadn't brought a translator; I'd been told one would be provided. My heart sank as I heard the cardinal begin to speak in Italian. I listened as best I could, and Rinaldi filled me in when the conference was over.

The cardinal continued:

> The imprint of the face and body of Christ on the shroud speaks eloquently of the solemn moments of his death and resurrection.... The exposition is an invitation to contemplate this unique image of Christ... to pay attention to the running blood of his body... to repent, worship, and give out with grateful love.... Christ was crucified on account of our sins; his blood was shed for our salvation; he has saved us with his passion.

When the cardinal finished his prepared statement, Cottino said that he would answer questions from the audience.

"Just how international was the commission that was formed in 1969 to conduct a secret investigation of the shroud?" asked Father Rinaldi.

Not as multinational as they would have liked it to have been, Cottino answered, and they hoped to add new members from other countries to the commission in the near future. "We will not be deaf to suggestions from others," he added.

When would the findings of this commission, which met four years ago, be released to the public?

"Be patient," said Cottino. "In a few weeks you will have all the news."

What progress had been made in fixing a date for the cloth?

Cottino rattled off the same objections to the Carbon 14 dating test that he had made to me, and then went on to add that according to Monsignor Pietro Savio, the Vatican archivist, the three-to-one herringbone twill of the shroud had been used by weavers in at least second-century Egypt.

I asked the next question: Were the 1969 photographs taken with ultraviolet light, and if so, did they reveal any marks or symbols not visible to the naked eye?

Only color film was exposed, said Cottino, and no symbols appeared on the prints that were developed.

Would Fortunato Pasqualino, began the next question, give his impressions of the shroud?

As if on cue, Pasqualino moved from the audience to the rostrum and stood next to Cottino; he was one of Italy's leading television personalities, and he would narrate the exposition on television. A large man with heavy, purple lips and a deep, rich voice, he said that he had never heard of the shroud before he was given the assignment to narrate the exposition. The best way of dealing with the question of the relic's authenticity, he said, was to approach it with a measure of skepticism. That way, the remarkable evidence in favor of its authenticity quickly comes into focus.

Suddenly and without warning—or was it entirely pre-arranged?—Cottino brought the press conference to a close by saying that everyone with proper credentials could view the shroud now if they would only follow him.

A MOMENT WITH THE SHROUD

Follow Cottino we did, down the open-air corridors bordering the huge palace courtyard and into the palace again.

About a hundred in all—news correspondents, local press, clergy, sindonologists—we climbed the broad marble steps curling up to the second floor, where two uniformed *carabinieri* stood in front of the Hall of the Swiss. The doors were open, and through them, thirty yards away against the far wall of the room, we could see the shroud. It was mounted vertically in a twenty-foot-high frame. We could see the man in the shroud standing in full front view; the back view was balanced, as it were, on top of his head.

At first, the group kept its distance. Then some began to inch toward the images. Afraid that the authorities might stop me from taking photographs, I hung back for a moment. I loaded my Nikon 35mm as inconspicuously as possible. An American sindo-nologist, Father Adam Otterbein, was doing the same thing. "I'll swap my black-and-whites for your colored shots," he whispered. I winked back, and we both started shooting.

Scaffolding had been erected against the wall facing the shroud; the television cameras would be operated from here. The pipes were already studded for the occasion with high-wattage lamps. From the scaffolding I got shots of the shroud and the crowd gesturing beneath it. Then I clambered down and, moving closer to the shroud, shot individual aspects of the images—the lower body on the frontal image . . . the large bloodstain on the wrist . . . the wound in the side . . . the face.

Since the authorities didn't seem to mind the cameras—a few others were clicking away too—I elbowed my way through the crowd to a spot about four feet in front of the relic. Suddenly it dawned on me that the glass in front of the relic wasn't reflecting any light. The television lamps illuminating the shroud were bright, even blinding, and by now I should have seen them reflected in my viewfinder. I reached out and, instead of touching glass, I felt fabric. I was touching the shroud.

How odd! Any one of the roughly one hundred people in the room could set a match to the shroud, or rip it to shreds with a knife, or throw a bomb at it—and no one else in the room would be able to stop him!

However curious I was about the reason for no glass, I didn't think long on it. I put another roll of film in the camera. But just as I raised the viewfinder to my eye, an official announced that time was up; the private showing was over, and all would have to leave. I continued to shoot until a monsignor tapped me on the elbow and told me to stop. Reluctantly, I stuffed the camera back into its case and followed the group out of the hall. Next stop: to see the silver-covered wooden casket in which the shroud is kept.

The Shroud's Casket

From the end of the sixteenth century until 1997, the shroud of Turin was kept wrapped cylindrically in a wooden casket covered with silver and jewels. But following a 1997 fire in which it was rescued from almost certain destruction, the linen was moved to a safer container. Today, in the industrialized area of Turin, it is laid out flat in St. John's church in a hermetically sealed casket specifically designed to shield it against water, fire, and pollution damage.

■ ■ ■ ■ ■ ■ ■ ■

Later, back at the hotel, I collected the impressions of the English and American sindonologists, most of whom had just seen the shroud for the first time.

Father Rinaldi, who had seen the shroud in 1933, said he was much more impressed this time. "Looking at the black-and-white photographs for so long, I had come to believe that the cloth was a maze of light and dark contrast. But in truth it is very clean-looking—like ivory—and the imprints are shadowlike. They fade . . . imperceptibly . . . into the cloth."

Everyone agreed that "imperceptible" was the appropriate word to describe the delicacy of the image.

"Black-and-white photographs give the impression of an altogether more bloody and damaged piece of linen than is in fact the case," said one Englishman. "This arises almost entirely from the fact that pale brown takes on a heightened definition and intensity when translated into black and white. You may have discovered the same effect if you have ever had old sepia photographs copied in black and white; the rejuvenation is startling."

I agreed with him. The body images were sepia, but the bloodstains were a different color.

"Carmine" or "carmine-mauve" were the terms three Englishmen used to describe the stains. "Carmine-rust" was preferred by two Americans.

And so the comments of the professional sindonologists continued.

THE SHROUD ON TELEVISION

Friday night was clear, and Turin bustled with traffic as Father Rinaldi and I tried to hail a cab. We and the other sindonologists had been invited to view the exposition at the local television station. By the time we got the cab, we had been joined by Monsignor Giulio Ricci, archivist at the Vatican's Congregation for Bishops and the highest-ranking Vatican prelate with active interest in the shroud. I had first heard of Ricci in 1968 in a *Newsweek* article. I met him in 1971 when I did my first story on the shroud, and had found him most cooperative. A plump, ebullient man with darting, sparkling eyes, Ricci was not at all like the secretive Catholic authorities I had had to deal with so far. In the cab he promised to help me again in any way he could.

Perhaps the most interesting deduction Ricci had made when I interviewed him in 1971 was that the man in the shroud had worn the robe first mentioned in John 19:23 and later made famous in a novel and movie. After Jesus had been scourged, said Ricci, a robe must have been flung over his shoulders. The flagellation marks that the robe or tunic would have covered—back, chest, and upper arms—appear smudged on the shroud; whereas the marks that were not touched by the tunic—such as the lower arms and legs and the face—appear decidedly more distinct. This phenomenon is especially visible, said Ricci, on the shoulders, where, all sindonologists agree, the man in the shroud carried a heavy, rough beam.

"If the cross Jesus was made to carry had been in direct contact with the lacerated shoulders, the lacerations would have been widened, forming large sores. But, on the contrary, they have kept their shape. This would not have happened without the presence of a robe protecting the shoulders already wounded by the scourges."

Another Ricci observation concerned the crown of thorns.

The fact that the bloodstains show that the man in the shroud wore a cap of thorns rather than a circlet is interesting, he said, and for more reasons than we have already stated. In the Western world we think of a crown as a circular band, like a wreath. But this was not true in the Orient. In the Orient, they always used a miter, a cap—a complete cap that enclosed the entire skull—when crowning a king. Thus, the marks on the skull, indicating a cap rather than a wreath, are not only a deviation from the traditional depiction of the crown of thorns, but are also in line with what would have been done in the East where Jesus' shroud would have originated. This is further evidence of the shroud's authenticity.

The cab deposited Ricci, Rinaldi, and me in front of the Italian national television office. Sleek and low, the building was in sharp contrast to the heavy eighteenth- and nineteenth-century structures that made up so much of Turin's skyline. Inside, plush carpeting swept down long corridors past glassed-in control rooms. Short-skirted women hurried in and out of doors. This must be Fellini's Italy, I thought, as we were met by a gray-flannelled young executive who ushered us smartly down the rest of the corridor to the widescreen projection room.

Live, from the Hall of the Swiss, came the first exposition of the shroud in forty years. The basic scene was of the shroud mounted in its frame on the wall, with Fortunato Pasqualino on one side of it and a gallery of the faithful on the other. Pasqualino narrated, while the camera moved in with close-ups of the shroud or panned the crowd of invalids, children, and the aged in the gallery, who appeared to be drawing some solace from the relic.

Also on the set, sitting in the middle of a line of altar boys, was Cardinal Pellegrino. He prayed; the gallery responded.

A videotape of priests taking the shroud casket from the shroud altar and then lifting the shroud from the casket was shown, as well as a reconstruction of the probable 2,000-year history of the shroud itself. Pope Paul VI, who rarely allowed himself to appear on television, spoke for eight minutes by videotape.

And that was that.

Austria, Belgium, Portugal, and Spain, by way of their national television systems, brought the program to their populations. As a consequence, perhaps as many as 200 million viewers saw the show, the largest audience ever assembled for a shroud exposition. They had sat through thirty-five minutes of pious devotion to what must have seemed to many of them, who had never heard of the shroud, to have been nothing more than a religious cloth with a strange painting on it.

Clearly, to the sindonologists who had come to Turin for the exposition, the event was a disappointment. True, they had

A Word from His Holiness

Paul VI was not the first pope to praise the shroud. Between 1472 and 1480, Sixtus IV issued four bulls indicating that he believed the shroud to be worthy of the highest veneration. In 1506, Julius II proclaimed the "feast of the Holy Shroud," with its own Mass and office, for the town of Chambery, France, where the shroud was located at the time. In 1582, after the shroud had gone to Turin, Gregory XIII extended the feast to the entire realm of the House of Savoy. Since Savoia extended at that time into France and the diocese of Troyes, this Mass was being celebrated in the very diocese where, two hundred years before, the shroud had been denounced as a fake. Between Gregory XIII and Paul VI, nineteen other popes expressed confidence in the authenticity of the shroud.

Pius XII, in a message to the First International Shroud Congress held in Rome in 1950, "wished that the participants at the congress contribute ever more zealously to spreading the knowledge and veneration of so great and sacred a relic." John XXIII, on seeing the shroud, was overheard saying, "This can only be the Lord's own doing." And Paul VI, in the course of a homily given during a Mass in St. Peter's Basilica, June 1967, said, "Perhaps only the image from the holy shroud reveals to us something of the human and divine personality of Christ."

gotten to see the relic firsthand, and true, more people than ever before had gotten to see the shroud, but the scientific aspects of the shroud were never mentioned. The Turin authorities later admitted that they had deliberately omitted them, because they didn't want controversy to mar the religious aspect of the event. Even the positive-negative aspect of the images on the cloth—the one thing that up until then set the shroud apart from all other ancient artifacts and relics—was glossed over.

"The distinct impression left was more reverential than enlightening," said Father Rinaldi immediately after the presentation was over.

No sindonologist he'd talked to since the telecast, said Dr. Judica-Cordiglia a day later, was satisfied with what had gone on the air. Judica-Cordiglia apparently was a member of the secret 1969 commission, and he was disappointed that he hadn't been consulted about the format of the program.

ON TO PARIS

I left Turin the day after the exposition. I was disappointed but not discouraged. I had gotten what I came for—and indeed a good deal more. I'd had a firsthand look at the Turin authorities, in whose inept, if well-meaning, hands the shroud rested. I saw the shroud itself, an experience worth far more than contemplating the photographs. And I bought a set of the color photographs of the shroud taken in 1969 by Giovanni Battista Judica-Cordiglia. Plus, I had my own—the first color photographs ever taken by a photographer not connected to the shroud.

Paris was the first stop on my itinerary. There I hoped to find some new information on the fabric of the shroud. I had managed to glean the following basic information about the shroud fabric from various reports and studies:

After studying the blowups of the 1931 Enrie photographs, textile experts were able to say that the shroud was made of linen woven from flax, a wiry, long-stemmed plant that grows best and most abundantly in sandy, temperate zones like Palestine. The flaxen threads, which appear coarse and were probably handspun, correspond to the No. 50 and No. 70 threads of the present-day English flax count. The pattern of the weave was an overall herringbone twill, broken at intervals by a forty-thread stripe.

Linens woven in 4000 B.C. can be seen in Egyptian museums; twill weaves existed long before the birth of Christ. But why wasn't there an example of herringbone twill dating back just 2,000 years? A relatively sophisticated loom would have been needed to do the job, some experts believed, and such a loom could easily have been invented by the time of Christ. Egyptian murals showing looms almost as advanced as required date back 4,000 years, other experts countered, and 2,000 years was more than enough time for loom technology in Palestine to develop sophisticated herringbone twill.

I hoped my investigation in Paris would yield more information about the ancient linen. In particular, I was eager to discover whether the textile aspects of the shroud would be helpful in determining how the images were formed.

I hoped Paris, a center of Egyptology and textile museums, might yield some answers.

CHAPTER 7

■■■■■■■■

FACE VEILS AND VISIONARIES

EGYPTIAN DEATH SHROUDS

● ●

My *first stop in Paris was* the Musée Guimet, a medium-sized building which housed a special collection of Oriental artifacts. According to a plaque inside the front door, the museum was founded in 1879 and became part of the Louvre complex in 1945.

At the front desk, I asked to see the Gayet collection. Yes, a curator said, there had been an archaeologist named Albert Gayet; yes, he had directed excavations in Egypt near Antinoe around the turn of the century; yes, the excavations had been financed by Emile Guimet...

"Is there any chance of my seeing the collection today?" I interrupted.

"No," he said. "At least not here at the Musée Guimet. The Gayet collection has been transferred to the main Louvre building."

"How far away is that?" I asked.

"About a mile."

I headed for the door.

"Try the Coptic section of the Egyptian collection," he called after me.

■■■■■■■■

I had first come across Gayet in a pamphlet on textile aspects of the shroud authored by the aged Vatican archivist and apparently indefatigable sindonolgist Monsignor Pietro Savio. What was especially impressive to Savio was the variety of ancient sophisticated weaving patterns, the herringbone among them, dating back approximately to 130 AD.

"The weaving industry was large-scale and fundamental to the economic and social life of Egypt," wrote Savio. Young people were paid to learn weaving, apprenticeship lasting sometimes as long as five years. The best fiber came from Acacia in the region of Elis. It took, on average, three men and one woman six days to weave a roll of cloth 98 feet long. The cloth was then boiled—presumably a cleaning process—and then dyed with colors extracted from herbs. Purple apparently was the most fashionable color, with natural "whitened with a kind of soap made from the poppy" as the second favorite. The finished product carried the name of the region in which it was manufactured, the most prized being Pelusium linen, and it was exported to a number of other Mediterranean countries that could afford to pay the price.

■■■■■■■

I had never been to the Louvre before, and so I was unprepared for what I saw looming before me: a U-shaped fortress many football fields long, built on the right bank of the Seine. In 1793, after the French Revolution, it was converted into a museum, which today houses such treasures as the *Venus de Milo* and the *Mona Lisa*.

I gave my name and purpose to a guard inside the front door. In a few minutes I was in the department of Egyptian antiquities, which had been started in 1826 to house collections acquired by Napoleon during his Egyptian campaigns. Then I arrived at the office of the Coptic section.

As usual, neither of the two women in the office spoke English. I tried my best to communicate with them in basic English, with gestures, and finally by drawing pictures of corpses with veils over their faces. At last they understood; one of them telephoned her boss and handed the instrument over to me.

It was Pierre Bourguet speaking; he was the curator. Yes, he did speak English. No, he couldn't see me today; it was his day off. After telling him in detail why I had to see him, he said he would make an exception to his usual holiday practice of "no work" and come down. I was to wait in his office.

■■■■■■■

I was looking for the Gayet collection because, in Turin, a British Benedictine had shown me Gayet's *Annals*, a copy of which he happened to have with him, and read me page 134.

"Among these documents," Gayet had written about the shrouds he'd unearthed, "the most important one is a face veil, folded in four, and carrying the impression of the face to which it was applied. These imprints formed something like dark spots where the prominences of the face were, and show up black.

According to the specialists, they are from the action of the chemicals used in the embalming of the body. This image gives us the face of a dead man."

The passage was accompanied by drawings of two of the dead bodies that Gayet had dug up. They had been wrapped first in shrouds and then mummy-style, apparently with the face veil having been applied first.

If the reference was correct, then I could locate another shroud with a body imprint and thus dispel the idea that the Turin shroud was unique.

■■■■■■■■■

Bourguet arrived an hour and a half later. He was a spry-looking man, bald, smoking a thin brown cigar.

After introductions—I was surprised to learn he was also a Jesuit priest—I asked him if he had ever come across a burial cloth with the impression of a face on it.

"No, never."

"What about the burial cloths in the Gayet collection?"

"I know the Gayet finds, but none of them have the imprint of a face. I'm sure. I would know."

I handed him the page from Gayet's *Annals*.

"It does say that here, doesn't it?" He sounded genuinely surprised. "Apparently there's something to what you say. But I've been through all the Gayet findings, and I've never seen a face veil."

Bourguet read the page from the *Annals* again. He looked at me for a long moment, then said, "It isn't normally done, but in view of the evidence I suppose I should do it."

"Do what?" I asked hopefully.

"If you'll come back tomorrow, I'll take you back into the storage room where they keep the reserves. You and I will go through all of Gayet's things, and that way we'll know for sure."

Of course I agreed to come back, and I thanked him for his courtesy.

■ ■ ■ ■ ■ ■ ■ ■

The Louvre truly was huge.

Two city blocks, five hundred yards, we walked—Father Bourguet with his secretaries and I with my camera and notebooks—through one hall after another of the enormous museum, passing by paintings of crotchety men, bosomy women, dreamy cloudscapes, and angry seascapes before we finally arrived in a gigantic room stacked to the ceiling with boxes and trunks. Cold winter air descended from a hole in the ceiling—the roof was being repaired—and dust rose as Bourguet pulled Gayet's trunks from the wall racks. Dark, moldy, bulky, there were three of them.

We carried the first, coffin-style, to an uncluttered spot under the hole in the ceiling (the light was best there) and opened it. It was full of burial cloths made of heavy, scratchy linen that looked like nightshirts or summer dresses. Actually they were tunics—simple, knee-length garments with sleeves to the elbow, no pleats, a hole for the head, and two side seams. Decorations of some sort had been sewn on some of the sleeves and bottom hems.

There were probably seventy-five such tunics in the trunk, together with some modest headdresses and small napkin-sized pieces of cloth. All, according to Gayet, had been used in burying Jesus' followers in Egypt, the Coptic Christians, around the end of the first century. The bodies had been clothed in the tunics, it appeared, wrapped in shrouds like the one in Turin, then wound mummy-style with ribbons of cloth.

Going through the ruins—I was tempted to hold my nose, but after 2,000 years there was no smell—I was immediately struck by the decomposition. Stains, looking like the swirls of what were once oil chemicals, went through the fabric to the other side. I thought I could distinguish bloodstains from decayed-flesh stains, but now I wasn't so sure. The tunics and the napkins had contained bodies all right, but there wasn't one imprint of a body or face. It was as though the bodies had simply melted through the cloth, leaving behind only a hodge-podge of human disintegration.

"You see," said Bourguet as he closed the lid of the first trunk, "nothing."

We moved on to the second trunk, and then the third. As he and I paid special attention to the napkins, which were the size of facecloths, the two secretaries "oohed" and "aahed" over the fabric, commenting excitedly on the weaves and strengths of the ancient linen.

"I didn't think you'd find one," said Bourguet as he closed the lid on the third trunk. "Now at least you know it's not here."

"At least the cloths prove that corpses buried in linen leave behind stains of decomposition," I managed to say.

"Why is that important now?" Bourguet asked.

"The shroud of Turin," I said, fumbling with my equipment.

"I'm afraid I don't know as much about the shroud as I should."

"Would you mind if I took some photographs of the burial shirts?"

"Go ahead. But please hurry before we all freeze to death!"

As I focused my lens on the swirls and stains, I couldn't help but wonder why the shroud didn't look the same. The body had been in the linen long enough to form an image on the cloth, but not long enough for the putrefaction now before me on the tunics to set in. I could only think of two reasons why.

Either the body, dead or alive, was taken or stolen from the tomb before decomposition, and the shroud left behind.

Or the body, dead but not having begun to corrupt, became alive again, shed the shroud, and left the tomb.

The first is a logical possibility; the other is a matter of faith.

But what about the blood clots, which Vignon, Barbet, and others studying them have noted are so picture perfect? If someone had stolen the body, the clots would have been messed when the cloth was separated from it.

It was a tough problem. As Vignon had noted, it seemed only the New Testament and science fiction offered explanations.

■■■■■■■

Later, back at his warmer office, Bourguet said, "There's only one more thing you can do. Some of the Gayet collection was sent to one of the two museums in Lyons where Monsieur Guimet, the man who financed Gayet, was from. You might go there. I know the curators. I could arrange things for you."

"I might just do that."

"But again," he said, "I don't think you'll find this imprinted face veil you're looking for."

"Why not?" I asked. "It, or something quite like it, must have existed in 1902 when Gayet wrote that passage in the *Annals*."

"If it did exist, and because it was such an unusual item, perhaps Guimet gave it away. He was the kind of man who, when somebody appreciated something, would say, 'Take it.'"

"Perhaps."

"As for Gayet, I know little about him. He may have been perhaps a little misguided, a little anxious, in describing the veil as having the imprint of a face. An archaeologist always needs justification for his funding, you know, and maybe Gayet, after a hard day's work, a little wine—"

We both laughed.

"But who am I to speculate on such things," he said with a grin. "If you want to go to Lyons, I'll be glad to make the introductions."

I decided against it.

"I have to be in London tomorrow. Perhaps I'll write to the museums. All I need to know is if they have such a face veil and can they send me a photograph of it."

■ ■ ■ ■ ■ ■ ■ ■

The decision to write rather than expend time and money on the extra travel turned out to be a prudent one. I got letters back from R. de Micheaux, curator of the Musée Historique des Tissues, and Madelaine Rocher-Janneau, curator of the Musée des Beaux-Arts, saying they were sorry, but there were no face veils in their collections of Gayet material. Michaeux went on to say that he would have been surprised if there were, since everything of Egyptian origin "had been sent back to the Louvre."

THE GERMAN DISSIDENT

When Kurt Berna, a German sindonologist and the man responsible for blowing the secrecy of the 1969 shroud commission, heard that I was researching the shroud for a book, he insisted on flying from Stuttgart, Germany, to London, to give me his several theories. On my own flight to London from Paris, I decided to sift through what I'd gathered on this man to see what I could learn before meeting with him.

First, it turned out, his real name was Hans Naber. For a variety of reasons he occasionally also used Kurt Berna and John Reban.

Hans Naber, so far as I could tell, had been born a Catholic, but his Catholicism was more a formality than a commitment. In 1936, when he was fifteen, he left school to learn the hotel business from the bottom up. He waited on tables in the restaurants of Europe—he once served Winston Churchill in London—but before he could advance from table waiter to *maitre d'hotel*, Hitler had advanced on Poland.

Drafted into the German army, Naber showed a talent for writing and became a reporter-writer for his company, a job which consisted mainly of writing up internal matters for the unit.

He was sent to France and took part in the battle of Normandy. When the German army was thrown into disarray by the advancing Allied armies, he deserted, escaped capture by changing clothes, and made his way back to Stuttgart.

After Germany's surrender, most Germans had to scrounge for necessities. Naber was no exception; he turned to black marketeering, which made him a modest living until 1947, when, he says, Jesus appeared to him in a dream.

Around 4:00 a.m. on February 18, 1947, lying awake in his parents' home, Naber saw on the wall of his bedroom a Technicolor "film of the passion." Included in it were scenes of the trial, crucifixion, entombment, resurrection, and ascension. "They were so real," he later told a magazine, "that I was under the impression they were actually happening. It went on for seven days. I couldn't eat or sleep. The only thing I could do was drink water. I couldn't get out of bed."

On the seventh day, with Naber "physically exhausted and on the verge of madness," something even more unusual happened.

"On one wall of my room, at a stroke, a very intense light appeared, and it diffused through the whole room. Within it Jesus appeared. . . . He was tall. . . . He had long hair, a beard, a mustache. . . . It was highly clear light, eerie, but at the same time not blinding, permitting a clear vision of him. He was dressed in a long white tunic, and there were no wounds on his body."

What Jesus said made such an impact on Naber that he picked up a pen and wrote it down as though someone were guiding his hand. In essence, the message was as follows:

I did not die on the cross.... The wounds on my hands and feet took away my strength. The pains burned in my body.... The beast opened up my side.... Its lance was thrust from below into my chest [but] it did not hit my heart.... My side bled.... My body was lifeless, but not dead. The heart still beat...my wounds were anointed with balm...Joseph of Arimathea laid me in a grave of rocks...my body could rest...my heart grew stronger...then I rose again.

While Jesus talked to him, Naber wrote on the paper. He said he could recall each item in vivid close-up, the most vivid of which were Jesus' last words: "I am Jesus whom men crucified. You, Hans, have seen that I did not die on the cross. You must render testimony of this fact." Then Jesus was gone.

Naber slept for three days and, revived from the ordeal, quit the black market and began giving fervent witness to the truth he believed he'd learned. *Neuen Zeitung*, an occupation-army newspaper put out by the Americans for German civilians, published an interview with Naber. Most readers didn't take the story seriously; some readers were outraged to think Naber would challenge the fact that Christ died on the cross.

He needed proof, Naber said, and not long thereafter he heard of the shroud of Turin for the first time.

■■■■■■■■

HANS NABER AND LEONARD CHESHIRE

HANS NABER

• • • • • • • • • • • • • • • • •

When *Naber and I met in London* the following day, he filled me in on what had happened next. A priest friend gave him a book on the shroud by R. W. Hynek, the Czechoslovakian doctor who had done work on the possible causes of Christ's death. When he came to the doctor stating that all doctors who have studied the shroud photographs at length believe it held a corpse, he stopped.

If the shroud had wrapped a dead man, he realized, then his vision couldn't be true. He would have to admit he'd been imagining things, perhaps even hallucinating. Naber couldn't accept either of these conclusions, so he bought all the books he could find on the shroud, as well as life-size blow-ups of the 1931 Enrie photographs.

Poring over the apparent bloodstains on the shroud, he told me, he suddenly recalled an incident in the war. "It was in 1942. On the home front. There'd been an automobile accident in which a man in our company had been killed. As the company writer, I was to go to the autopsy with my sergeant. The doctor made a cut on the man, but no blood came out. I was surprised and asked the sergeant why this was so. He said he didn't know. We asked the doctor, and he said corpses don't bleed. They can bleed a little— a few drops maybe, but not large quantities.

"And so, while I was looking at the shroud pictures and all the blood on the shroud, I remembered what the doctor had said. Corpses don't bleed. And then I realized that there was my proof. The body on the shroud was covered with blood! Yet corpses don't bleed! The body must not have been a corpse. It must still have been alive when put in the shroud. Otherwise, how could the blood have gotten on it? Corpses don't bleed. The heart must still have been pumping when they put Jesus in the shroud!"

Later Naber qualified his statement. Corpses, as the doctor had said, could bleed a little, but not in the amounts shown on the shroud around the scalp and on the hands and arms. Such copious exudations, he said, could only have been pumped out by a living heart.

Still later, Naber received confirmation of this theory from another doctor, W. B. Primrose, former senior anesthetist at Glasgow Royal Infirmary. In an article entitled "Jesus' Survival from the Cross," Primrose used, among others, the argument that corpses don't bleed.

Reflecting on his seven-day vision, Naber made another determination. He had seen the tip of the lance, which was thrust up into Jesus' right side, sticking out of the left pectoral muscle.

In other words, according to his vision, the lance tip had not come to rest within the chest cavity as most historical, medical, and theological experts believed; it had emerged several inches above the left nipple. Peering at the pectoral area on his shroud photos, Naber even thought he could see the tiny wound mark. It was circular and could be differentiated from the marks of the scourging, which were straight and smaller.

By drawing a straight line from the point of entry on the right side between the fifth and sixth ribs (according to Barbet's hypothesis, which was quoted by Hynek) through the lungs to the exit wound at the left pectoral muscle, Naber had what appeared to be a lance-path that missed the heart. He promptly went to a hospital where he had an X-ray taken with a simulated lance laid across the course he'd plotted. The result was a negative of his chest cavity with a lance-path that missed the top of his heart by approximately three inches.

Now there was no question in his mind that his vision had been correct in all its details. He began to search for other supporting evidence, especially in the Scriptures. "Nowhere in the Old Testament does it say that the Messiah had to die, or would die, on the cross," he said, and in support of this he cited

> ## Why Did God Forsake Him?
>
> The Gospel describes Jesus agonizing just before his death: "And going a little farther he fell on his face and prayed, 'My Father, if it be possible, let this cup pass from me; nevertheless, not as I will, but as thou wilt.'"
>
> —Matthew 26:39

verses from the fifty-third chapter of Isaiah. Nor did the New Testament indicate that Jesus wanted to die. To prove this, Naber cited Matthew 26:39.

Salvation came at the ascension, theologized Naber. The resurrection was really just resuscitation. Christ may have appeared dead when he was taken from the cross, but in reality he was still alive. His breathing and other life signs may have stopped, but enough oxygen was still circulating in his blood to keep vital centers, such as the brain, alive. Once in the tomb, the calm allowed him to revive.

AIRING HIS VIEWS

By the mid 1950s, Hans Naber ran into stiff opposition while trying to get his theories accepted in Germany. "Purest fantasy" is what Werner Bulst called them; he was a Jesuit priest and professor of fundamental theology at a Catholic college in Frankfurt, and one of the few scholars in Germany at the time writing in support of the shroud's authenticity.

In 1954, Naber told me, he put his theories into book form, calling it *The Fifth Gospel*. He managed to borrow money to get it printed, and sent copies to the Vatican. The average German reader, however, refused to buy the book; it was a flop.

Around 1955, Naber met a 75-year-old pathologist from Cologne who agreed with his theories. Hirt was the professor doctor's name; Naber couldn't remember his Christian name. Together they created "The German Convention for the Shroud of Jesus" in 1956, and from that time on Naber would refer to this "convention" as a body of scientists who agreed with his findings—although he seemed to be the only vocal member.

By 1960 Naber had written a second book and published three profusely illustrated magazines. At first glance these magazines could easily have been mistaken for European editions of well-known mass-market periodicals, so professionally and glossily had they been put together. A glance at the mastheads inside, however, identified Naber himself as editor-publisher.

Waging a campaign against what he considered falsehood in Naber's writings, Jesuit Werner Bulst wrote in 1960: "An uninformed reader might perhaps treat as important the fact that in his reports [Naber] frequently refers to well-known authorities such as Prof. Dr. Von Campenhausen [Professor of Protestant theology at Heidelberg], Prof. Dr. Siegmund [Catholic theologian of Fulda], and Prof. Dr. Reisner [a physician from Stuttgart]. Personally questioned [however], all declared that they had no connection with [Naber] or his ideas." Bulst's book, *The Shroud of Turin*, respected amongst sindonolgists, was published in the United States in 1957.

Around 1960, Naber told me, he met a rich banker. He wouldn't identify the man other than to say he was a jeweler from Switzerland who believed that Naber's theories were a possible bridge between Jews and Christians. If Jesus hadn't died on the cross, so this man's thinking went, then the Jews couldn't be blamed for his death. This immediately became a recurrent theme in Naber's writing.

In 1964, Naber founded "The International Foundation for the Holy Shroud." He refused to reveal the foundation's membership, he said, because they would be subject to unfair attacks from powerful Catholic sources, but he did use the foundation to raise money for his work.

The next year, under the name of Kurt Berna, he published a book entitled *Inquest on Jesus Christ*; it was subsequently translated into English and published in London. Probably as a result of this book, the success and notoriety for which he had been working the past eighteen years came suddenly. A UPI wire story, dated November 22, 1967, flashed his story around the world. (This was the story that had first alerted me to the shroud.) Soon, in addition to the one in Stuttgart, Naber opened offices in London and Zurich.

In "Did He Die on the Cross?," an essay in a 1967 issue of the *Ampleforth Journal*, a British Benedictine publication, David Willis took issue with several of Naber's theories. Willis was a doctor himself, latest in a long line of distinguished British physicians. In the seventeenth century one of his ancestors, Thomas Willis, was credited with both having discovered diabetes and with giving his name to that arterial network at the base of the brain now known as the circle of Willis.

With regard to corpses bleeding after death, Willis quoted in the course of his essay Dr. Derek Barrowcliff, British Home Office pathologist:

> It can be demonstrated in the mortuary that a short stab wound or cut on the back of the scalp comparable with the wounds made by the crown of thorns...or indeed a cut into any dependant part, will bleed freely, continuously, unimpeded by any of the natural mechanisms such as spasm of blood vessel or clotting of the blood which in the living would tend to arrest bleeding. Blood will flow from an open vein as long as the normal laws of gravity operate upon the hydrostatic pressure.

As for the lance missing the heart, Willis said that Naber had calculated incorrectly the exact location of the entrance wound. He asserted:

> It is meaningless to say a wound is in the space between the fifth and sixth ribs without qualification because there can be a difference of 6–7 inches in height between the front and back of the space due to the downward slope of the ribs. The entrance wound as it appears on the shroud is clearly at the front of the rib slope, and if Naber had only realized that, his simulated spear thrust would definitely have hit the heart.

With regard to a photograph used in Naber's *Inquest on Jesus Christ*, Willis charged forgery. Naber claimed the anatomical diagram which he used was a diagram of an adult human heart, while in reality it was the diagram of a young child's chest cavity. The reason why the Naberian spear would have missed such a heart is that the organs were not fully grown.

Willis went on to say:

> The piercing of the heart is irrelevant because the executioners—Roman soldiers trained in the art of using their weapons and well qualified to know when death had ensued—were convinced that their work was complete in the case of his companions; otherwise they would have broken Christ's legs as they did in the case of the two robbers. The piercing of Christ's side, then, was in the nature of a coup de grace, not the finishing off of someone half dead.

Following the appearance of the Willis essay, Naber admitted in an interview that several of the photographs in *Inquest on Jesus Christ* had been retouched. On photographs of the blood, he had darkened the stain considerably, in an attempt to boost the credibility of his theories. He hadn't done it to deceive anybody, he said; the original blood on the body, and indeed on the shroud, must have been much darker, and he wanted the photographs in his book to conform to what actually had once been the case.

Also in 1967, Naber's foundation came under attack by the United States for mailing a brochure appealing for money to a women's organization in Trenton. The women turned it over to the Better Business Bureau of Central New Jersey, who, with the aid of the chancery office of the diocese of Trenton, queried Swiss Church officials. The reply from Zurich was anything but flattering: it called the International Foundation for the Holy Shroud a "hoax."

■■■■■■■

It was Naber who exploded the secrecy of the 1969 shroud commission—he said he had been tipped off by an official in Turin who wished to remain anonymous. On June 16, the first day of the study, Naber sent out leaflets and releases charging that the Church was going to alter or destroy the shroud. Naber wanted to protect the shroud because he was convinced that it proved his theory that Christ did not die on the cross. News media in Turin and Rome picked the story up and sent it out over the global wire services. The Vatican quickly denied the charges, and the story seemed to die down.

On June 28, ten days after the secret study had been completed, Naber showed up at the Vatican gates with a briefcase full of documents and a photographer. Monsignor Charles Moeller, undersecretary of the Vatican's chief agency concerning doctrine, may have been extending the courtesy of the Vatican when he invited Naber inside the complex, but when he was photographed accepting Naber's documents, the story went global.

"Vatican City," United Press International (UPI) started its article.

The President of the "Foundation for the Holy Shroud in Switzerland" submitted documents to the Vatican which he said prove Christ was alive when removed from the cross. Prof. Kurt Berna said in the documents, accompanied by photographs of the shroud which reputedly was Christ's burial sheet, that marks on the shroud were caused by fresh blood.... This contradicts the belief of the Roman Catholic Church. It would mean that Christ recovered from wounds and did not rise from death itself. There was no comment from the Vatican....

The Associated Press (AP) story had the same tone and substance:

> A German author who contends Jesus Christ did not die on the cross has challenged the Vatican to reexamine the shroud believed to have wrapped Christ's body.... Kurt Berna, author of four books on the shroud, says bloodstains on the cloth prove Christ was still alive when taken from the cross. He went to the Vatican yesterday and gave a 20-page pamphlet containing photographs and what he called documentation to the Rt. Rev. Charles Moeller.... The Vatican made no immediate comment.

The story seemed to die down, at least for five months. Then, in December 1969, Naber got another tip from a source he refused to identify; a high Vatican official was reputed to have said that "the Holy Church cannot be split and teach that our Lord Jesus Christ died on the cross to free us from our sins, and at the same time worship a shroud in which no corpse ever lay. A radical solution must be found here."

Naber called the Zurich bureau of Reuter's, the English news service. The shroud is going to be destroyed, he told a reporter, "for how else are 'radical solutions' to be understood?" Vatican officials had already tried to harm the shroud once, he added, and this time he had a quote to prove it. Reuter's, convinced of the reasonableness of his previous stories, sent this one to its subscribers around the world.

At last the Turin authorities were forced to admit what they had previously denied. On January 6, 1970, Cardinal Pellegrino released through his curia a short statement to the effect that, yes, the shroud casket had been opened; and that, no, the cloth had not

been destroyed; and that experts had been asked to make suggestions on how to preserve the holy relic for possible future studies.

Crucify Him!

So well known in all its horror was death on the cross to the first
Christians that they grasped at once all that was contained in the
evangelists' brief statement, "They crucified him." First century pagan
and Christian authors "assume familiarity" with the torturous execution method "and speak of it only in a few passing words."

The Persians probably started it. The Romans later adopted it from
their enemies, the Carthaginians, and made it the fearful punishment
for robbers, war deserters, traitors, rebels, and slaves. The punishment included scourging and carrying one's cross. The victims sometimes lived a day and night. Breaking of legs, which curtailed
breathing, was used to hasten death. Before death, the crucified victim, with weight sagging, was forced to push up on nailed feet in order
to draw air into the lungs. Victims were usually left on the cross to rot
or be eaten by vultures.

—From "The Archaeology of the Crucifixion," Rev. J. J. Collins, S.J.,
S.S.L, in the April 1939 *Catholic Biblical Quarterly*.

If 1969 was the zenith of Naber's credibility, 1971 was the
nadir. He was charged with defrauding creditors of $75,000. "You
must make a difference between the foundation and this charge,"
he told me. "In the early 1960s I wanted to publish another book.
But because no one would publish it because it was against the
Church, I had to publish it myself. I had to raise the money. There
were about twenty investors. I told them the book was going to
be a big seller. But it didn't sell so good and the publishing house

I set up—it was a little publishing house—it went broke. Afterward, the investors said I was not talking correctly with them. Maybe I did not say the risk, but how could I know the press wouldn't review my book. It was big stuff, but they wouldn't print anything about it."

He said he had tried to pay the money back, but one of the investors had him arrested. In 1972, he was found guilty on charges of fraud and was sentenced to two years in prison; he appealed the decision.

The 1972 Summer Olympics, held at Munich between August 26 and September 11, gave Naber an unhoped-for chance to air his views to the world. "Dear Sirs at the foreign press: attention! Germany has secret press censorship!" These were the first words of numerous packets he sent to the Olympiad Press Center.

> You are now in a perfectly organized country...so perfectly organized that discoveries of world significance, which were made in Germany, have now been censored in the German press for over 16 years and therefore not printed! Tell your country not only about the sport but also about the country and people you encounter here. Here are the facts.

No stories about him or the shroud seem to have emanated from Munich during the games. Even if the packets had elicited the attention of some of the journalists, the events of September 5 would have overshadowed them: eleven members of the Israeli team were killed by "Black September" terrorists, and news of the tragedy and its aftermath were headlines for days after.

Like Bulst in the 1960s, I had trouble confirming Naber's arguments from medical and biblical authority. Naber was most reluctant to give me names and addresses, and when he did relent,

I had little luck. Letters to the radiologist in Stuttgart who backed his claim that the spear would not have entered the heart, to the professor at the University of Tugingen who said that corpses don't bleed, and to the British publisher of *Inquest on Jesus Christ* were either returned, "addressee unknown," or went unanswered. The only one who replied was W. B. Primrose, the anesthesiologist from Glasgow; he still believed corpses don't bleed.

What is one to think of Hans Naber? The road he chose to take from 1947 to the present appears to have been one, not so much of deceit, as of a fierce belief that what he had seen in his vision was right, and of his overzealousness in trying to make others realize it. The obsession eventually stripped him of family and friends, threw him into collaboration with mysterious figures, and in the end turned him into a 300-pound, broken man facing bankruptcy and jail.

GROUP CAPTAIN LEONARD CHESHIRE

I next wanted to meet Leonard Cheshire, the man with the shroud bus, who once brought Josie Wollam, a 10-year-old victim of osteomyelitis, to Turin in 1955 in search of a miracle. An aerial bombing expert and crack pilot, he had been one of the RAF's "dambusters," pilots who volunteered to fly at low levels through almost impenetrable flak to drop 12,000 to 15,000-pound bombs on pinpoint targets, like the submarine pens at Le Havre and Bologne. For these and other deeds of courage and leadership, Cheshire was eventually awarded the Victoria Cross, the Distinguished Service Order, and the Distinguished Flying Cross.

He had been Churchill's personal representative at the dawn of the nuclear age, flying in the plane that dropped the atomic bomb on Nagasaki, Japan, August 9, 1945. The blinding white flash, the eerie purple glow, the evil mushrooming fire cloud—he'd witnessed it all first hand and returned to England to tell about the bomb that killed 80,000 people so that hundreds of thousands might live.

After the war, he decided to steer his life into what he felt was a more meaningful course. With a group of ex-servicemen, he organized a self-sustaining community. With nothing but brotherhood as its bond, and with little agreement as to their general focus, the community soon went broke; its members departed, and Cheshire himself fell ill.

To recuperate he went to the Canadian Rockies, and some time during his convalescence he underwent a religious experience. He described this experience as awe at the wonderfulness of creation.

Returning to England, he decided to open a home for the terminally ill. His first patient was Arthur Dykes, a man dying of cancer. They became good friends, and they discussed religion incessantly. When Dykes finally died, Cheshire, reasoning from the laws of aerodynamics to the doctrines of theology, decided to become a Catholic. The Catholic Church, he'd decided from the discussions with Dykes (a believing Catholic), was the "true Church," the rightful inheritor of Christ's message.

That was 1948. By the mid-1950s, encouraged by support from the press and donations from the people, Cheshire's home for the terminally ill incorporated as "Mission for the Relief of Suffering" and opened two more homes. Once again, though, Cheshire overworked and fell ill, this time with tuberculosis. He was confined to a sanatorium for eighteen months. It just so happened that an image of the man in the shroud was affixed to the wall of his room.

■ ■ ■ ■ ■ ■ ■ ■

I had arranged an appointment with Cheshire, but when I called later to confirm it, I learned that he was out of town. An aide said that he'd written to cancel the appointment, but unfortunately the letter never caught up with me. To make up for the missed appointment, John Messent, deputy clerk of London's Metropolitan Water Board and a good friend of Cheshire, offered to meet with me and fill in details of Cheshire's life. This is what I learned:

Recuperating at the sanatorium, Cheshire contemplated the man in the shroud. He had read a pamphlet on the shroud written by an American and had found the scientific facts intriguing. He grew to feel that his new-found ministry and the shroud had something in common; both dealt with suffering—the one to relieve it, the other to make its significance understood. He decided to write a pamphlet himself, one aimed specifically at the English reader.

He decided also, on his discharge from the hospital, to buy a bus and convert it into a mobile shroud museum. From G. Enrie he ordered an enlargement of the positive of the frontal view of the body; when it arrived from Turin, he had it enlarged to life-size and installed it over a light panel on the floor of the bus. He then wired an amplifier that would play Gregorian chant and hung cages for doves that could be released at appropriately pious moments. With these and other sindonological paraphernalia he embarked on a tour of England, lecturing on the relic and giving away copies of his pamphlet.

Churchmen may have winced at Cheshire's tactics, but newspapermen rejoiced at the war hero who had been charmed by a religious relic. HOLY SHROUD GIVES SILENT WITNESS IN LONDON ran one headline. V. C. TELLS THE STORY OF THE SHROUD read another. During the week before Easter 1954, two thousand Londoners passed through the bus, and ten thousand copies of the free pamphlet had been scooped up.

Cheshire himself wrote a story for *The Daily Sketch*, entitled "I Saw the Face of Christ."

In addition to recounting the pertinent facts, Cheshire wrote that he was more impressed with the shroud than with the atom bomb. The shroud may look like just another portrait, and the bomb appeared destined to change the course of history; yet the shroud loomed higher on his own horizon because "here at last might lie the secret to world peace."

■■■■■■■■

The next day I traveled to Nottingham to visit D. Allen-Griffiths, a 71-year-old secretary of the Holy Shroud Information Center, another of the English groups interested in the shroud. Griffiths had written a book on the shroud, *Whose Image and Likeness?*. He was especially helpful in giving me additional details of Cheshire's pilgrimage to Turin with Josie Wollam in 1955.

THE INVALID AND THE SHROUD

When Josie, a 10-year-old victim of osteomyelitis, heard of the shroud in 1955, she asked her parents if she could see the real thing. Perhaps it could cure her twisted leg, stop her internal hemorrhaging, and dry the running abscesses on her skin. "I'm suffering like Jesus, aren't I?" she asked her mother. "If I am blessed with the relic, I know I'll get well."

The girl's full name was Josephine Wollam, and she got in touch with Cheshire, who was touring with his shroud bus at that time. Cheshire went to visit Josie and decided to try to make the girl's wish come true. He didn't know how he would be able to get in to see the shroud, but perhaps Josie would succeed where scholars and sindonologists had failed. Almost before travel arrangements could be made—the tickets were delivered to them on the railroad platform—he and Josie set off first for Cascais, Portugal, to get King Umberto's blessing on the undertaking.

By the time they arrived in Turin, the press had got wind of the mercy mission. Josie and Cheshire were met at the train by reporters, photographers, priests, and several representatives of the king; Umberto had already telephoned his approval of the mission. Apparently the king's influence was nil, however, for when the entourage arrived the following morning at the cardinal's residence, Fossati was not inclined to see them. However, when he heard that Josie had brought with her a white dress made especially for the occasion by her mother, he telephoned the Vatican for permission.

It was 4:15 p.m. when they entered the cathedral through the side door and went up the steps of the Chapel of the Holy Shroud. The doors were bolted and locked behind them. Only the cardinal, some priests, the guardian of the shroud, two nuns, and the king's representative were present with Josie and her sponsor; the press had been allowed to deceive themselves into thinking that the private exposition would take place that night.

When Josie returned from the sacristy where she had gone to change her dress, the cardinal beckoned her to his side. He was kneeling in front of the shroud altar. A moment of silence and prayer followed; then the cardinal gave the signal. Two priests approached the altar, climbed up the steps to the vault over the altar, and unlocked the three devices on the safe. They reached inside and brought out a long, slender, embroidered casket, and with the help of two more priests, they carried it down and deposited it on a table next to the cardinal.

Another moment of silence, another prayer, then the casket was placed in Josie's lap. When nothing of a miraculous nature seemed to happen, the casket was put back on the table. Josie looked up to the cardinal as if to ask if she could see and touch the shroud itself.

The cardinal huddled with the priests around him. Then he examined the seals surrounding the casket and even tried to pry open the lid without breaking the seals. When unsuccessful, he sent for a pair of scissors, cut the silk tapes and opened the lid.

The two priests reached inside and brought out the shroud, which was encompassed in red silk affixed with yet another set of seals. Gently, they placed the shroud against her twisted leg. A profound silence settled upon the chapel. When nothing happened, Josie looked at the cardinal again. He told her she could put her hand inside the silk covering, but there was nothing else he could allow her to do.

As the shroud was replaced in the casket and the casket restored to its vaulted shrine, Josie and her patron prayed. On leaving, she told the cardinal she felt better, and the cardinal reportedly looked pleased.

No miraculous cure had ever been attributed to the shroud of Turin. Nothing unusual occurred during Josie's first visit, nor during another one a year later. But how can one explain the fact that as Josie grew older, her health improved? By the early 1970s, she had married and started a family of her own, showing no signs of her former illness.

CHAPTER 9

■■■■■■■■

ANCIENT IMAGES, CRUSADER MONKS

HOLY ICONS

● ● ● ● ● ● ● ● ● ● ● ● ● ● ● ● ●

To find out more about the history of the shroud before the 1350s, I planned to call on two British sindonologists. The first was Father Maurus Green; he was the Benedictine who had given me the reference in Gayet's *Annals* in Turin. His father, Charles Green, was a career army officer and amateur sindonologist, who had developed the iconography theory already put forth by Paul Vignon. According to his theory, the shroud face had been the model for many early Christian icons.

When the elder Green died in 1959, with his manuscript on the subject as yet unpublished, the younger Green, now a parish priest, decided to pick up where his father had left off. In time he came to know as much about the shroud's probable history as any sindonologist alive. And when in 1969 his "Enshrouded in Silence," a lengthy article examining all the evidence contributing to the history of the first millennium of the shroud, was published in *Ampleforth Journal,* he was recognized as the foremost expert in the iconographic aspect of sindonology.

Briefly, the iconography theory was this:

As mysterious as the shroud was, the face it displayed was remarkably similar to the traditional image of Christ seen on many ancient icons, the religious paintings of early Eastern Christianity.

The first depictions of Jesus were highly idealized; he was shown as a clean-shaven, innocent youth. Around the sixth century, however, that image changed. He suddenly became a grown man with long hair, beard, and eyes that were abnormally large and ovate. If someone had copied the shroud face, the eyes would have appeared exactly that way.

Art historians don't know exactly why Jesus was depicted in these two contrasting ways. Nowhere in Scripture is there any physical description of Jesus; several apocryphal works do contain some random and contradictory descriptions. Could the shroud, then, have caused the change in the way artists portrayed Jesus? Could it even have been the model upon which the virile icons were based?

It was an intriguing idea, one first expounded by Vignon in 1902 and fully developed by him in his second book, *The Holy Shroud of Turin Versus Science, Archeology, History, Iconography, and Logic,* published in Paris in 1939.

Checking the icons in the museums and libraries of Paris, Vignon discovered dramatic evidence that the shroud face and the face on the icons had more than a casual link to one another. Not only did the eyes, nose, and mustache appear the same, but strange marks that were not facial features also appeared on the faces in both the shroud and the icons. The most unusual of these is a mark between the eyes, just above the top of the nose. It resembles a V with a rectangular box resting on top of it; the box appears to have one of its sides, the side nearest the hairline, missing.

This unusual, non-anatomical mark appeared in several different forms. On the earliest icons, such as the one in the St. Pontianus catacomb in Rome, which dates back to the sixth or seventh century, it appears as the box with one side missing, but it does not have the V. On the icons made in the eleventh century, such as the Christ of Daphni in Greece, the mark is more stylized; the rectangular lines have become a teardrop or a pendant.

Of the hundreds of Byzantine icons Vignon examined, 80 percent had the identifying mark between the eyes. Among other points of similarity, Vignon listed the following: no ears; no neck; no shoulders; a "forked" beard; a "truncated" mustache; straight nose; enlarged nostrils; one raised eyebrow; a line across the throat (which is really a wrinkle on the shroud); bruised forehead; abnormally shaded or swollen cheeks. No icon had all these similarities, but all had at least a few.

THE MANDYLION

The earliest icons Vignon found with similarities to the shroud were copies of the "Image of Edessa," a portrait of Jesus on cloth which was discovered in 544 bricked up in a wall in Edessa, the center of Syrian Christianity. After its discovery, the "true likeness" of Christ (as it came to be known) was the object of great veneration in Byzantium.

"Edessa must be the key," Father Green said when we met. "If I could search hard enough and a good deal longer, I believe I could come up with more evidence showing that the shroud had been in Edessa. This would give more credence to Vignon's theory, give me something to finish off my father's book, and advance the cause of the shroud in the process."

In a 1937 article, Vignon had written:

There are many representations of Christ, notably the Image of Edessa, which could be derived only from the shroud. A careful study of these copies, which I recently completed, shows that the ... face visible on the shroud served as a model for artists as early as the fifth century. The artists did not copy slavishly, but tried to interpret the face, translating the masklike features into a living portrait, which was still a recognizable copy of the original.

In 1938, Vignon published his second book (referred to above), an updated revision of his 1902 work on the shroud. As convincing as the arguments in his book were to many, scoffers at the authenticity of the shroud still pointed to the lack of an unbroken chain of documents attesting to the shroud's existence before 1354.

"The more I dug," Father Green told me, "the more convinced I became that I would not find any more references to Christ's shroud than had already been uncovered. The documents had been pretty thoroughly sifted. There just didn't seem to be anything substantially new I could find. But the Eastern preoccupation with icons—the preoccupation that caused the exaltation of the Edessan image and gave rise to the subsequent mass of Byzantine Christs—still bothers me. Why had the Eastern Christians been so impressed with images when Christians in the West had been content with relics? It was then that Ian Wilson [the other British sindonologist I planned to meet with] came along with his intuitive theory: the Edessan image had not been just the first copy of the shroud, as Vignon theorized; it had been the shroud itself!"

Green told me he fought tooth and claw against this theory at first. All scholars know that the Edessan image is only a portrait of Christ; at least that's the way the evidence has always been treated. But then again, he began to realize, it was a cloth, and it had been greatly exalted after its discovery. Perhaps the scholars were wrong.

"The more my friend Ian Wilson and I exchanged information on the subject and argued back and forth, the more I realized how this theory might possibly be the missing clue to the puzzle. So many things were pointing to the icon of Edessa. And the more facets I studied, the more probable the theory became."

The theory that the Image of Edessa was the shroud began with legends. In essence, they say that when an early king of Edessa, Abgar V, became mortally ill, he sent for Jesus, the miracle-worker he had heard about. Jesus did not go to the king himself; instead he pressed a cloth to his face, miraculously leaving his image on it, and sent that back with the king's messenger. The cloth not only healed Abgar; it also converted many of the citizens of Edessa to Christianity. Shortly thereafter, a Roman army invaded the country, but the Image of Edessa, as it was now being called, had already mysteriously disappeared.

When the icon was discovered hidden in the city (now Urfa in Turkey) in 544, it was proclaimed the greatest relic in Christendom. *Acheiropitos* they called it, a Greek word meaning "not made with hands"; it was also called "The True Likeness of Christ." Placed so as to guard the city, the cloth was said to have miraculous powers in repelling attackers. Eventually it came to be known as the *mandylion*, a Greek word for cloth or veil. Three or four copies of it were made at the end of the sixth century and—after the defeat of iconoclasm, the great movement to destroy images, which flourished in Byzantium in the eighth and ninth centuries—the image spread throughout the empire.

By the tenth century, the image had become so revered that Romanus Lecapenus, emperor of Byzantium, decided he wanted it in the treasure chests of his palace in Constantinople. He sent an army to the gates of Edessa to bargain with the Moslems who were currently occupying the city. The army's instructions were that if they couldn't get the image by bargaining, they were to get it by battle. Outnumbered, the Moslems agreed to relinquish the image in return for two hundred Moslems then being held captive, and for twelve hundred silver coins.

The mandylion was brought to Constantinople in 944 amidst great fanfare. Accounts say the cloth was marched triumphantly around the city walls, then taken ceremoniously through the "golden gates" to be lodged permanently in the imperial chapel of Bucoleon. In some accounts, the mandylion is termed a "shroud." Fittingly, in 1150, a shroud began to be listed among the prizes in the city's treasury; and an anonymous English pilgrim listed the shroud—not merely a facial imprint of Christ—as one of the treasures in the emperor's chapel. Was this the mandylion? There are also two recorded references—one made in 1171 and the other in 1201—to a shroud in the Bucoleon Chapel. In 1204, the Fourth Crusade sacked Constantinople, and the Image of Edessa disappeared again.

Green said that he happened upon three pieces of documentary evidence indicating that the Image of Edessa also had a body imprint on it, giving more credence to the idea that it actually was the shroud now in Turin.

"That changed the situation considerably," he said.

"The first document is a reference from a sermon about the Edessan Image believed to have been given by Pope Stephen III, who was elected to the papacy in 769." The text of the sermon, by the way, appears in a copy made sometime between the ninth and twelfth centuries.

The sermon first says, in a passage that may have been added long after the pope's death, that the image impressed on the cloth is Jesus' body.

> For the same mediator between God and men... stretched his whole body on a cloth, white as snow, on which the glorious image of the Lord's face and the length of his whole body was so divinely transformed that it was sufficient for those who could not see the Lord bodily in the flesh to see the transfiguration made on the cloth.

Then the sermon identifies the body imprints on the cloth as the Image of Edessa. "This cloth, despite the passage of time, remains incorrupt in Mesopotamia Syria in the city of Edessa in the house of the great church."

Green said the second and third documents are references from twelfth-century authors. In 1142, Ordericus Vitalis, discussing the origin of the icon of Edessa, wrote the following: "Abgar reigned as Toparch of Edessa; to him the Lord Jesus sent... a most precious cloth, with which he wiped the sweat of his face and in which shone the image of the same savior marvelously depicted; which exhibited to the onlookers the likeness and extent of the body of the Lord."

A short time later Gervase of Tilbury, in discussing a letter Jesus is alleged to have sent to Abgar, quoted Jesus as saying: "I send you a cloth in which the figure of my face and my whole body are contained."

"These are just fragmentary references of course," said Green, "and not very impressive by themselves. Vitalis and Gervase are generally considered by most medieval historians to be gossipers. But then Ian Wilson found the only official history of the Edessan Image ever commissioned, had it translated into English, which

had never been done before, and again, the results were support-
ive of the theory that the image and the shroud are one and the
same."

The Hymn of the Pearl

In an ancient poem, Jesus describes himself as he appears on the
cloth at Edessa:

But all in the moment I faced it
This robe seemed to me like a mirror,
And in it I saw my whole self
Moreover I faced myself facing into it.
For we were two together divided
Yet in one we stood in one likeness.

Interestingly, this description applies perfectly also to the shroud
of Turin, which bears two images, one of the front and the other of the
back, of the man portrayed.

De Imagine Edessa, as the history was entitled, was written by
a member of the court of the tenth-century emperor, Constantine
Porphyrogenitus, shortly after the image arrived in Constantinople. Its pertinence to the shroud comes in a short description of
how the image on its surface appeared to be composed: "...a
moist secretion without any coloring or artificial aid."

"Clearly," said Green, "this brings us very close to the same
apparent characteristic of the Turin shroud. Ian [Wilson] has also
highlighted the importance of an incident recorded in 944," he continued, "when the emperor's sons had a special viewing of the
image. To the sons it seemed blurred, but Porphyrogenitus was an
artist; he was able to make out the portrait clearly. Something of the
subtlety of the Turin shroud's stain image is again suggested here."

"But if this were all so," I asked, "why had all the references to the Edessan Image almost overwhelmingly indicated that it had nothing more than a facial image on it? And why had so many copies of it shown nothing more than a facial image on it?"

"Good questions," said Green.

MORE ON THE EDESSAN IMAGE

"Did the image of Edessa have body imprints on it?" This was the question I posed to Ian Wilson when I first met him in Turin. He was an Oxford history graduate and an enthusiastic sindonologist.

Wilson replied to the effect that a Greek liturgical text of the tenth century told how the cloth was so highly venerated and so closely guarded that few were ever allowed to view it directly. The cloth was kept in a casket (very similar to the container in which the shroud is kept now), and people were allowed to see this casket only through a grille (again, very similar to the situation of the shroud today). Only on very solemn feast days was the archbishop allowed to open the casket and view the image for himself. Nobody else was allowed to open it. It was never there for just anybody to see, as it were. And these would have been just the circumstances for the full-length figure to remain secret.

Further, Wilson went on to say, another text refers to the mandylion as having been "doubled in four." He said he took a full-length photograph of the shroud, doubled it in four, and the result was that only the head showed. "If that's how the image was folded," he said, "then even if the entire casket were opened, no one could have seen the body image."

This reminded me of something else Father Green had told me while I was still in Turin. "There's another piece of evidence," he said, "the Byzantine liturgical cloths called *epitaphioi*. . . . The still-surviving epitaphioi are liturgical aids dating from the thirteenth century that have the dead and reclining Christ embroidered on their surfaces. Many of them have the figure in the exact same position as the one on the shroud. Jacques Grimaldi, writing in Latin in 1618, suggests that the earliest epitaphioi were known as far back as the eighth century."

"Once the Edessan Image reached Constantinople in 944," Wilson continued, "the evidence that it and the shroud are the same increases. Both Christ's burial garments and the Edessan Image are said to have been kept in the Bucolean Chapel. In 1201, a palace priest, Nicholas Mesarites, indicated that one of the relics kept in the Bucoleon shows the naked body of Christ. And then in 1204, Robert de Clari, the chronicler of the Fourth Crusade, the one that leveled Constantinople, wrote that he had seen the shroud of Christ in the city and that it had the imprints of his entire body on it."

And then there are the Vitalis and Tilbury references, I thought.

Were the Image of Edessa and the shroud of Constantinople the same? And were they both the same as the shroud of Turin?

No one can be sure, it seems.

Father Green had become convinced that the two images were the same, however, based on a comparison of the shroud of Turin with the Holy Face of Laon, a mandylion painted around 1200, perhaps directly from the Image of Edessa. Green was sure that the Holy Face of Laon was inspired by the shroud face, and therefore that the artist knew the shroud face well, whenever he saw it.

The chief difficulty with this theory, everyone admitted, is that both the Edessan Image and the burial cloth of Christ are sometimes mentioned as separate and distinct entities on the same lists of relics in twelfth- and thirteenth-century Constantinople. The difficulty can be explained away, said Wilson, by suggesting that the Edessan Images mentioned in the lists are just copies of the original, and that therefore the orig-inal, which would have the body imprints on it, could have been what the lists referred to as the shroud.

"If Wilson is right," Green later said to me, "we will not only have solved the mystery of the Turin shroud's whereabouts during the first millennium, we will also have a most remarkable account of its by-no-means-inconsiderable place in Byzantine history."

"If you are both right," I said, "then only one historical mystery remains. What happened to the shroud between the time it disap-peared in Constantinople in 1204 and reappeared in Lirey, France, around 1356?"

The answer, it seemed, had to do

> ### Nicholas Mesarites Speaks of the Shroud, 1201
>
> "In this chapel Christ rises again, and the sindon with the burial linens is the clear proof...the burial shrouds of Christ: these are of linen. They are of cheap and easy to find materials, still smelling of myrrh and defying decay since they wrapped the outlineless, fragrant-with-myrrh, naked body after the Passion."
>
> —Nicholas Mesarites
> *Die Palasrevolution des Johannes Comnenos*

with the storied Knights Templar, the mysterious Crusader monks about whom there is much controversy.

WARRIOR MONKS

The Knights Templar, as I later learned, were a religious and military order that had been started by a small group of Crusaders in Jerusalem around 1119. Eight or nine of the knights who had been fighting in the Holy Land decided to drop out of their indi-vidual armies and form a religious order. Tired of the secular lives they had been leading, they took, in addition to a vow to protect pilgrims from attacks by marauding Moslems, vows of poverty, chastity, and obedience, and adopted as their dress a white sur-coat with a red cross in the middle. They pooled all their posses-sions and gave a tenth of everything they acquired to the poor. They swore to take on no fewer than three foes apiece in any one battle.

Apparently, other knights and mercenaries in increasing num-bers felt the same way as the original founding group, because within fifty years the order had become a large and powerful army. Money poured in, both through dowries of new members and fees for the Knights' martial services; little money trickled out. No leader of any army dared antagonize them. Within their own fortresses, the Templars were practically self-sufficient. In time they became the Western Church's arm in the East, and in 1163 the pope gave them the right to establish their own clergy. They became like a nation unto themselves.

Toward the end of the twelfth century, however, things changed. The founding knights had all died. The vows of war and chastity were still sworn to, but the order's wealth was being invested in real estate all around the Mediterranean world: in Jerusalem, Tripoli, Antioch, and Cypress in the East; in Spain, France, Portugal, and England in the West. "At their peak," wrote one historian, "the Templars owned and administered seven thou-sand manors and estates in Europe."

By 1200, the Templars were the dominant power in the Middle East. Their strongholds along the African coast and on up through the underbelly of Europe were said to be impenetrable. They established friendly ties with some of the Arab armies. Some Moslems even trusted the Templars enough to bank their valu-ables in the Templar strongholds. In 1204, the armies of the Fourth Crusade (including Templars) sacked Constantinople—and the Shroud of Constantinople disappeared.

So was the Image of Edessa the same thing as the shroud of Constantinople, which then became the shroud of Turin?

"I've found no direct evidence linking the Templars to the shroud," Ian Wilson told me in Turin, "but I do have three pieces of circumstantial evidence."

First, in 1307 the Templars, too strong and independent for the European monarchs' taste, were brought to their knees. The king of France had all the Templar leaders in his realm arrested on the charge that they secretly worshipped a mysterious idol "in the form of the head of a man with a long, reddish beard." The idol was never found, but Wilson said he couldn't help but see a resemblance in that description to the face on the Turin shroud.

Second, a painted head, believed to have been a replica of the idol the Templars might have worshipped, was found on the site of an old Templar monastery in England. "Its resemblance to the shroud face," Wilson said, "is unmistakable"

Third, as a result of the purges in Europe, three Templar leaders were burned at the stake. One of the last two to be incinerated was a French Templar named Geoffrey deCharnay. The shroud would come to light in the church of another Geoffrey de Charny in Lirey fifty years later, in 1354. Although the last names of the two Geoffreys were sometimes spelled differently, Wilson said he believed they were related.

What about the d'Arcis memorandum? I asked. (This was the 1389 document written by Bishop Pierre d'Arcis alleging that the shroud had been found in 1356 to be a painted fake.)

"The whole d'Arcis affair was just a big mistake," Wilson said. "The bishop was a sincere man, but he misinterpreted the facts."

When deCharnay, the probable descendent of the Templar whose order had been purged and disbanded fifty years earlier, was killed at the Battle of Poitiers, fighting for the French, his wife may have put the shroud on exposition with the hope of making a little money. The local clergy probably found it hard to believe that such a tremendous relic could have come into the hands of a modest secular family, and without the former owner around to explain where he got the shroud and exactly what its history was, they branded it a fake.

"I believe that too much effort has been put into discrediting the d'Arcis memorandum," said Wilson. "The truth of the matter is that virtually all his facts were truthful and indeed valuable; it was his interpretation that the shroud was a fake that was misguided."

Beyond that, Wilson wouldn't elaborate. "You'll have to wait for my book to come out," he said.

The rest of the history of the shroud is a matter of record, and undisputed. The d'Arcis memorandum proved the shroud was still at Lirey in 1389. The imbroglio left the shroud intact, and in 1452 Geoffrey deCharny's granddaughter Margaret sold it to the House of Savoy.

▪ ▪ ▪ ▪ ▪ ▪ ▪ ▪

So much for the known history of the shroud, I thought. I headed for New York. The textile evidence I had seen so far was convincing. But I was looking forward to talking at some length with the American sindonologists and to doing some investigating on my own into the possible origins of the shroud images.

CHAPTER 10

■■■■■■■

THE SHROUD
IN AMERICA

FATHER EDWARD W. WUENSCHEL

● ●

My *first stop back in the United States* was Mount St. Alphonsus Redemptorist Seminary in Esopus, one hundred miles up the Hudson River from New York City. In a room next to the seminary library is the largest collection of sindonalia in the world outside of Turin. On the walls are life-size (7' x 4') photographs of the shroud; on pedestals and tables are pieces of sculpture modeled on the figure in the shroud; and in the bookcases are seven hundred volumes, mostly in French and German, although some sixty are in English. Also in the room are three file cabinets, four drawers apiece, full of un-catalogued notes, articles, manuscripts, and correspondence of the first great American sindonologist, Edward. W. Wuenschel.

Wuenschel entered the Redemptorists in 1913, was ordained a priest in 1924, received a doctorate in sacred theology in 1927, and returned to Esopus to teach dogmatic theology shortly thereafter. In the 1930s he was a voluminous writer and much-sought-after lecturer. In 1947 he was appointed rector of the seminary; in 1949 he went to Rome, where he headed the Redemptorist graduate school; in 1960 he became special theological adviser to Francis Cardinal Spellman for the Second Vatican Council, which was to convene in 1962.

When Wuenschel first learned of the shroud in 1934, he was skeptical. After reviewing the evidence, however, he became an ardent supporter of its authenticity. He was the one who, in 1937, arranged for articles to appear in *Scientific American, Reader's Digest,* and *Look*. These presentations of the case for the authenticity of the shroud were not satisfactory in every respect, according to others, but they did manage to introduce the shroud to portions of the American public who would not have heard of it otherwise. In the 1940s Wuenschel researched Jewish burial practices and published his results in the *Catholic Biblical Quarterly*. In the 1950s he spent the summers traveling to the European cities important to the history of the shroud and rummaging through bookshops for any and all material concerning it. After his death— he died without ever having seen the shroud—his notes and acquisitions from this time were shipped from Rome to Esopus and now form the basis of the Wuenschel Collection at the seminary.

From the files of the Wuenschel Collection, I learned many things, the two most interesting of which were, perhaps, his relationship with an editor at *Scientific American* and his discoveries about what happened to the shroud between 1354 and 1452. When Wuenschel first wrote to *Scientific American* about the possibility of an article on the shroud and enclosed all the positive scientific evidence in favor of the phenomenon, the letter fell on Albert Ingalls' desk.

Ingalls' special interest was not religion, but the telescope—how to make one, how to grind the lens, how to use it to explore the heavens; by the time of his death in 1958 he had written the article on telescopes for the *Encyclopedia Britannica*, and a lunar crater had been named in his honor. When he opened Wuenschel's letter, he smiled and rejected it politely, with the comment that miraculous intervention in the imprints on the shroud would not be acceptable to his agnosticism, let alone to his magazine.

Undaunted, Wuenschel sent a second letter in which he detailed all the negative arguments against the shroud's authenticity, asked Ingalls to consider them, and expressed confidence that he would find them unconvincing. Wuenschel also promised that the article, if *Scientific American* would publish it, would deal only with natural causes.

Ingalls was impressed enough with Wuenschel's second letter to reread the first. In it he noticed, as if for the first time, the argument from photography, which intrigued him as a scientist. He replied to Wuenschel that, although he'd like to commission an article, he couldn't see his way to publishing a piece that would be considered propaganda for the Roman Catholic Church.

Wuenschel wrote back, saying he agreed entirely with the editor's observations. A scientist—Paul Vignon—would write the article, and the verifiable photographs of Giuseppe Enrie would illustrate it. To give Ingalls some idea of the visual impact of the shroud, and to assure him of his own impartiality, Wuenschel invited him to a lecture featuring the Enrie photographs, which he would soon be giving in the auditorium of St. Vincent's Hospital in Manhattan.

Ingalls accepted, attended, and apparently was impressed enough to read the French original of Paul Vignon's 1902 book on the shroud. On the basis of the photos and the book, he at last badgered his editor in chief into commissioning the shroud article. It would run three pages in the magazine; *Scientific American* would print a disclaimer on the first page of the article; Vignon and Wuenschel would receive a hundred-dollar fee.

When the article finally appeared in the March 1937 issue, it was a great success. The shroud's existence was broadcast to perhaps 100,000 educated American laymen (most of whom were Protestant or agnostic), and Ingalls became an ardent defender of the shroud's authenticity.

■ ■ ■ ■ ■ ■ ■ ■

Showing Some Leg

In June 1937, on the heels of the ground-breaking, favorable article on the shroud appearing in *Scientific American*—due entirely to the efforts of American sindonologist Fr. Edward Wuenschel—*Look*, a newer and more sensationalist picture magazine than *Life*—ran unauthorized 1898 Secondo Pia photos of the shroud. Father Wuenschel, Turin's authorized representative in America, was incensed. Not only had *Look* not gotten permission from him, which he felt had been purposely avoided, but the new magazine, instead of using the newer and better 1931 Giuseppe Enrie photos, had retouched the "imperfect" Pia photos, "deforming" them more, in Wuenschel's words. Worst, the magazine had scandalously displayed the sacred photographs opposite what Wuenschel deemed a "pornographic" feature showing a pretty girl hiking her skirt! It was "one of the lowest and meanest tricks of crooked journalism," wrote the priest to *Look*.

To get more information on Albert Ingalls, I telephoned the offices of *Scientific American* and was put through to one of its editors.

"I hope you understand," the editor said, "that *Scientific American* is under new ownership now, and we certainly wouldn't have published that article today. It was nonsense."

"Why?" I couldn't resist asking.

"It's just too much to expect that a piece of cloth supposedly wrapped around a man in the Year One would still be a viable subject today. We have too many ancient cloths from Egypt to know this just couldn't happen."

"Ingalls believed the shroud a viable subject," I countered. "Otherwise, he wouldn't have gone to bat for it as he did."

"I knew Albert Ingalls very well," retorted the editor, "and I don't care what letters you have. I refuse to believe that he would have been responsible for an article like that."

"Have you ever read the article?"

"I read it several times, and I remember reading it as a sixteen-year-old boy and thinking how improbable the whole thing was."

"Have you read anything else on the shroud?"

"I'm familiar with the outlines of the story, and it's not worth exploring further."

Whoever the editor was—I didn't catch his name—his response to the shroud reminded me of some of the attitudes Vignon and Delage had encountered some seventy years ago.

■ ■ ■ ■ ■ ■ ■ ■

Also depicted in Wuenschel's correspondence was the success he'd had in unearthing the documentary evidence for the whereabouts of the shroud between 1354 and 1452.

He wrote:

> At Turin there was a woman on the staff who took a ferocious interest in my project and kept digging up material, the existence of which I did not even suspect.
>
> It was the same at Chambery. I had a letter of introduction to the Italian consul, who turned out to be the perfect diplomat and got me into the archives with the ease of a Ludwig von Pastor. There I had the whole staff at my command and permission to work in the archives after the closing hour. They also let me take jealously guarded books to my room at the Grand Seminaire.
>
> At Troyes I struck the best luck of all. I knew the old vicar general....He is one of the leading historians of Champagne...as familiar with the local archives...as with his breviary, and those are the archives that contain the most important collection of documents on the beginning of the Western career of the shroud—the whole Lirey story and its sequel....What a haul! I was able to do in three or four days what it would have taken months to do in the archives on my own.

What Wuenschel found seemed to validate Ian Wilson's theory of what happened to the shroud from the time it appeared in Lirey in 1354 until it was sold to the House of Savoy in 1452.

FATHER ADAM J. OTTERBEIN

When Wuenschel left the United States for Rome in 1949, he left the care of the American shroud movement in the hands of another Redemptorist priest. Adam J. Otterbein, a former student of his and a professor of theology at the seminary, was the one who shot the black-and-white photographs at Turin while I was shooting the color ones. Many was the night the tall, lanky Otterbein had listened to the chain-smoking Wuenschel as he pointed out detail after detail of the fascinating and mysterious relic.

Otterbein took his new assignment seriously, and for the next two years worked hard. On October 6, 1951, Francis Cardinal Spellman, then archbishop of New York, officially decreed the creation of the Holy Shroud Guild at Esopus, with Father Otterbein as its director. In December of that year, Turin approved the guild as its first North American affiliate of the Cultores Sanctae Sindonis, the parent organization. The guild was now the organization's official representative in the United States, with the responsibility of promoting interest in the relic throughout the country.

To attract members and inspire donations, the guild published a pamphlet containing all the pertinent facts about the shroud. The pamphlet was a reprint of *The Chalice*, a magazine published by the Confraternity of the Most Precious Blood, an entire issue of which had been devoted to the shroud in 1937. A former newspaper rewrite man created the pamphlet. Eye-catching headlines like "A Photograph of Christ" led to short, punchy paragraphs about the "linen cloth of ancient weave," "imprints made by the body of a dead man," and other compelling shroud facts; each page was illustrated with a photograph or a line drawing. By early 1954, 130,000 pamphlets had been sent out, according to the *Holy Shroud Guild Bulletin*, a mimeographed newssheet which the guild had started mailing out to its membership in June 1952. Active membership was approaching one thousand, with members in thirty-seven of the then forty-eight states.

In 1956, hoping to generate some new finding of his own, Otterbein visited the Eastman Kodak Company in Rochester, New York. The shroud, after all, was a photographic phenomenon of sorts, and he hoped that photographic experts would be able to shed new light on its mysteries. The Kodak executives were cordial, and they discussed the problem at a round table; but the best they could offer was a promise of help in planning another photographing session, should the shroud be shown publicly again.

Several months later Otterbein called on Dr. James Manning, head physicist-chemist at the New York City Police Crime Laboratory in Brooklyn. Without actually seeing the shroud itself, Manning couldn't say much; however, as Otterbein later wrote:

> He suggested a study or analysis of the cloth's weave. We pointed out that this had already been done.... Next he suggested the possibility of a chemical analysis to discover the substances which caused the stains. Then we had to point out that it was almost certain that chemical analysis would not be permitted because if the bloodstains were really the blood of Christ, it would not be fitting that this should be subjected to chemical analysis.
>
> Dr. Manning grasped the reasons which seemed to exclude direct chemical analysis and replied that there were several other possibilities; e.g., X-ray diffraction and microspectroscopy. He then explained both processes and indicated that they might reveal the presence of haemin crystals on the cloth. These microcrystals would make possible definitive identification of the stains as blood-stains. On the other hand, Dr. Manning told us that at least 96 organic substances in human blood have been indentified, and as soon as blood is exposed to the air, multiple and rapid changes take place. Hence, positive identification of the blood as blood would not seem possible except by reason of the haemin crystals.

Later that year, Otterbein visited the Federal Bureau of Investigation in Washington, D.C. The result was the same. They suggested how to test the cloth but could say nothing without seeing the linen themselves.

In 1957, Otterbein presented the shroud story on WBZ-TV in Boston. While the show was in progress, a crew from the archdiocese of Boston filmed it. The resultant 29-minute film was turned over to Modern Talking Pictures, a distribution company with offices in twenty-eight American cities. Thirty copies of the film were made, and MTP estimates that perhaps as many as 250,000 people—school assemblies, church groups, women's clubs—saw it before the prints wore out.

But perhaps Otterbein's greatest contribution was in helping remove a long standing bias against the shroud in the influential *Catholic Encyclopedia*, the major Catholic reference book in the English-speaking world. The bias was established by Herbert Thurston, a learned Jesuit who sided with Ulysee Chevalier in the debate sparked by the Pia photos.

Herbert Thurston, a British cleric, known at the turn of the twentieth century as an objective and searching writer of exceptional knowledge in the fields of history, liturgy, and hagiography, was one of the most influential people in the modern history of the shroud. As a result of his special interests, he would become expert in the occult, eventually writing books on mysticism, ghosts, and poltergeists. But he condemned the authenticity of the shroud in the 1912 edition of the *Catholic Encyclopedia*, and for the next fifty-six years anyone wanting quick and reliable information on the shroud in English read Thurston's badly misinformed article.

Thurston first attacked the shroud in 1903. In two long articles for *The Month*, a scholarly Catholic publication, he detailed everything that had been said against the shroud following Pia's photographs in continental Europe. He included the explanation that the shroud images had probably been produced by an accidental inversion of its colors through the centuries—a theory that had been refuted by Vignon. He felt that the fourteenth-century D'Arcis documents strongly indicated that the shroud was a painted fraud and that the absence of historical documentation before that time was proof enough that it was not genuine.

Thurston wrote:

> It appears to me quite conceivable that the figure of Our Lord may have been originally painted in two different yellows, a bright glazed yellow for the lights and a brownish yellow for the shadows. What chemist would be bold enough to affirm that under the action of time and intense heat (like the fire of 1354) the two yellows may not have behaved very differently, the bright yellow blackening, the brown yellow fading?

Because he never examined shroud photographs as Vignon had, Thurston relied heavily on Chevalier, who had also never examined them. Both clerics refused to accept Vignon's report that there was no paint on the shroud.

Some forty-five years later, another Jesuit priest, this time an American, took the first steps leading to changing Thurston's article. Having read what was the first favorable article on the shroud to appear in a standard Catholic reference work—the 1953 edition of the (Italian) *Enciclopedia Cattolica*—Walter Abbott reported its details (discussed below) in the April 1955 issue of the *American Ecclesiastical Review*.

The first part of the Italian encyclopedia article was written by Pietro Scotti, the priest-chemist who took part in the 1950 sindonological conference; he noted that providential circumstances had to occur for the blood stains to have been etched so perfectly on the shroud, and that the essential circumstance was certainly the resurrection. The second part was written by Alberto Vaccari, a Jesuit priest and Scripture scholar at the Pontifical Biblical Institute in Rome. Vaccari concluded that the Gospel of John was not in conflict with the existence of the shroud, as several Scripture scholars had maintained. This influenced English prelates, and shortly thereafter Walter Abbott himself wrote a heavily pro-shroud article for the supplement mailed to buyers of the English-language *Catholic Encyclopedia*.

It was not until 1968, however, that the Thurston article on the shroud was finally replaced in the encyclopedia itself. And it was Father Otterbein, by then known for his shroud activities, who was given the honor of writing the new article. Otterbein presented an evenly balanced statement of the facts as he understood them from his shroud mentor, Father Wuenschel. His article included a description of the cloth, various scientific studies that had been carried out with the help of the photographs, and discussions of the historical and scriptural problems. The entry concluded with the following paragraph:

> There are still many unanswered questions, but the accumulation of evidence from different fields of knowledge presents a formidable argument in favor of authenticity. The rapid progress of science and scholarship has made a new exposition of the shroud advisable.

Besides reaching the English Catholic reading audience, perhaps the largest in the world, Otterbein's article had a further impact. In the late 1960s the *Encyclopaedia Britannica,* because of the recent favorable coverage of the shroud, gave a few lines on the existence of the relic—something it had never done before—in one of its periodic updates. When the reference work was totally revised and published in 1974, it contained for the first time an article on the shroud, albeit only 120 words: "Shroud of Turin," read the entry, which was flanked by a photograph of the face, linen cloth purporting to be the burial cloth of Christ. . . . In 1898, the first photographic plates were made of it. . . . After studying this evidence two professors of biology presented to the Academie des Sciences in 1902 their conclusions. . . . The history of the shroud, however, cannot be traced beyond the mid-14th century.

The article, of course, was not entirely satisfactory to Otterbein, but at least the world of secular scholarship was beginning to take notice of the existence of the shroud and would presumably have to deal with it in the near future.

Why the Shroud Was Moved to Turin

In 1578, the Duke of Savoy moved the shroud to Turin, Italy, from Chambery, France. Hostilities between the duke and France, as well as his preference for the culture of the Turin area, factored into his decision. Also, St. Charles Borromeo, then the archbishop of Milan, wished to venerate the shroud in thanksgiving for Milan's survival of the plague. It is said the Duke wanted to save the sickly saint an arduous trek over the Alps from Italy to France. The shroud has been kept in Turin ever since.

FATHER PETER M. RINALDI

Assisting Otterbein with the Holy Shroud Guild was Peter M. Rinaldi, S.D.B. At the time of the 1933 exposition, Rinaldi was a Salesian seminarian, acting as interpreter for the many pilgrims and curiosity-seekers who visited Turin that year. The first magazine article of consequence on the shroud published in the United

States was written by him; it appeared in the June 1934 issue of the *Sign*, a national Catholic monthly. This was the article that had ignited Father Edward Wuenschel's lifelong interest in the shroud. Forty-one years later, Rinaldi would write again for the *Sign*. In the February 1975 issue, in an article entitled "I Saw the Holy Shroud," he gave his impressions of the 1973 exposition.

Through his interest in the shroud, Rinaldi touched another soul, Mrs. I. Sheldon Tilney. When she read Wuenschel's article in the March 1937 *Scientific American*, she became an ardent supporter of the shroud and eventually a convert to Catholicism. Ironic, perhaps, is the fact that her husband was secretary, and her brother president, of *Scientific American*.

"The Tilneys spent their winters in Palm Beach, Florida," Rinaldi recalls. "I was in Tampa at the time she visited me, and I arranged to give a number of lectures on the shroud, several to be at her home. One of those lectures, by the way, was attended by Mrs. Rose Kennedy [mother of President John F. Kennedy] and some of her children."

In 1940 and again in 1971, Rinaldi arranged for the publication of his own books on the shroud. The one in 1940 was *I Saw the Holy Shroud*, which sold almost 100,000 copies. The book in 1971 was *It Is the Lord: A Study of the Shroud of Christ* (which was published in paperback in 1975 by Warner Books).

In 1950, upon becoming pastor of Corpus Christi Church in Port Chester, New York, Rinaldi erected a shrine to the shroud with financial help from Mrs. Tilney. Though considerably smaller than the magnificent chapel housing the shroud in Turin, it was decorated with a marble statue of the body of Jesus, a mural depicting his burial, and a life-size transparency of the shroud's frontal image illuminated from the back. In 1970, the shrine was relocated to the side of the church, enlarged considerably, and enriched with mosaics and paintings. A later addition to the church was a crucifix with a life-size corpus. One of three fashioned by Monsignor Giulio Ricci, it has the more than one hundred flagellation marks that are discernible on the shroud.

THE POPULARIZATION
OF THE SHROUD

In 1963, Random House published *The Shroud* by John Walsh. Unlike most others who had written about the linen, Walsh was a professional writer, and consequently his book was a highly readable, informative, and objective account of the 1898 events, the 1931 exposition, and its immediate aftermath. In researching the shroud, he had conferred at length with Father Wuenschel and interviewed the surviving relatives of Secondo Pia, Paul Vignon, and Pierre Barbet.

Walsh stated in the preface:

Only this much is certain...the shroud of Turin is either the most awesome and instructive relic of Jesus Christ in existence—showing us in its dark simplicity how he appeared to men—or it is one of the most ingenious, most unbelievably clever products of the human mind and hand on record. It is one or the other; there is no middle ground.

Another vigorous sindonologist (whom I was never to meet) who presented the shroud story to middle America was Francis L. Filas, a Jesuit priest and professor of theology at Loyola University, Chicago.

In 1952, he persuaded executives of WNBQ-TV in Chicago to let him present the shroud story on Good Friday. They agreed. The 30-minute program ran at noon, and by 5:00 p.m. the station received four hundred telephone calls from viewers asking that the program be repeated. In an era when few people had television sets, this was an overwhelming response. Before the month was out, Filas had received 3,100 letters.

On Good Friday, 1954, the American Broadcasting Company televised the show to thirty of its network stations. Viewers in Illinois, Massachusetts, Florida, Louisiana, Missouri, Michigan, and some of the Rocky Mountain states saw Father Filas, in business suit and Roman collar, spotlight various details on the shroud photographs with a long wooden pointer. "Is the shroud authentic?" he asked and then proceeded to answer in the affirmative, providing as much evidence as he could. At the program's end, he told viewers that if they wanted more information, they should write to the Holy Shroud Guild, of which he was vice president. This time he got 13,000 letters.

By 1959, the shroud show was a tradition in the Chicago area. The ABC television network broadcast it to eighty-six different geographical audiences from California to New York, and *Time* magazine described it as one of the outstanding telecasts of the Easter weekend. In 1968, it was estimated that the show had drawn 150,000 pieces of mail. In 1974 Father Filas said that approximately forty-six million viewers had seen the program since it first began.

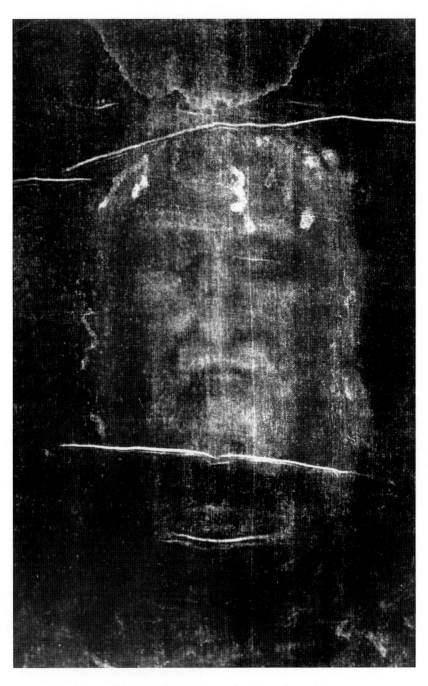

The face of the man on the Turin shroud,
believed by many to be the face of Jesus Christ.

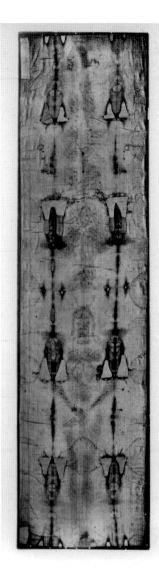 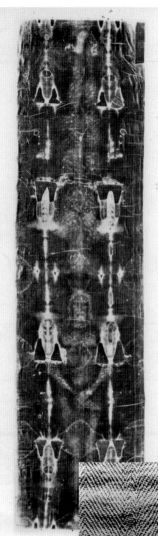

ABOVE: Full-length view of the shroud, one positive (left—as it appears to the naked eye), the other negative (right—as it appears on a film negative).

RIGHT: Close-up of the three-to-one herringbone weave of the shroud linen.

Ancient Roman nail, found at excavation site. Nails like this one would have fastened Jesus to the cross. This is also the type of nail believed to have been used on the man in the shroud.

Representation of the burial of Jesus by sixteenth century artist Giulio Clovio.
It is believed that the shroud enwrapped Jesus' body lengthwise,
as depicted here, which would account for the images on the Turin shroud.

ORATIONE DELLA SANTA SINDONE
OMNIPOTENTE sempiterno Iddio, il quale in memoria della Passione dell'unigenito tuo figliuolo ci hai lasciato la Santa Sindone con la sua espressa Imagine da esser adorata in terra, ti preghiamo a farne gratia che per virtù della medesima Santa Sindone meritiamo di contemplare la tua faccia in Cielo Amen.
IN TORINO Aprile Giouanni Tessa Con Priuilegio di S.A.R.

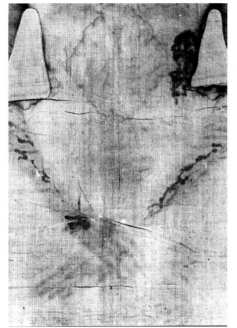

ABOVE: Italian holy card bearing a prayer to the Turin shroud.

LEFT: Enrie photograph of the nail wound in the wrist of the man on the shroud. Notice that the blood from this wound appears to have flowed up, though the arms are folded downward. This is because the arms would have been extended during crucifixion, and thus the blood from the wrists would have flowed down the arms from that position.

The shroud being prepared for the 1931 exposition.

The Shroud exhibited in Turin in 1931.

Outside view of the Cathedral of St. John the Baptist in Turin, Italy, where the shroud currently resides.

Close-up view of the ornate shroud altar in the Cathedral of St. John the Baptist. The shroud is kept behind an iron grating above the altar.

Full view of the shroud altar in the Cathedral of St. John the Baptist.

Photograph taken by the author during the 1973 showing of the shroud
which he attended. At the time this was one of the only
color photographs of the shroud in existence.

Icons bearing certain features of resemblance
to the face on the Turin shroud.

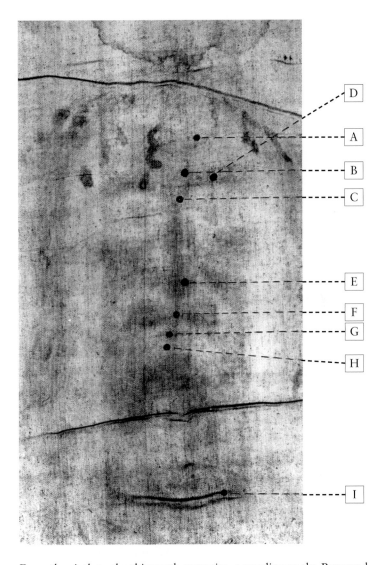

From the sixth to the thirteenth centuries, according to the Reverend Maurus Green, O.S.B., certain features in the representations of Jesus seem to indicate that the artists drew their inspiration directly or indirectly from the features on the shroud. Green particularly points to (A) the bruise across the forehead; (B) three sides of a square between the eyebrows; (C) V-shape to the bridge of the nose; (D) one raised eyebrow;
(E) enlarged nostrils; (F) divided moustache; (G) heavy line under lower lip; (H) gap between this line and the beard; and (I) the line across the throat. Compare these features on the shroud image with the corresponding ones on the icons on the opposite page.

Two American sindonologists, Father Peter M. Rinaldi (left)
and Father Adam J. Otterbein (right), holding a
photographic reproduction of the shroud.

LEFT: Paul Vignon, pioneer in the study of the shroud.
Credited with the vaporograph theory and the iconograph theory.

RIGHT: King Umberto II of Savoy, former owner of the Turin shroud.

Wood engraving of Jesus raising up the
daughter of Jairus (Luke 8: 54) by Gustave Doré.
Photo: © The Granger Collection

Josie Wollam, a 12-year-old victim of osteomyelitis, and Group Captain
Leonard Cheshire. Cheshire, a war hero and expert on the shroud,
took Josie to Turin in 1955, hoping for a miraculous cure for the little girl.

Joe Marino with his wife, Sue Benford. Benford and Marino
co-authored the influential paper, "Evidence for the Skewing of the
C-14 Dating of the Shroud of Turin Due to Repairs."

View from behind the altar of the interior of the
Cathedral of St. John the Baptist in Turin, where the shroud is kept.

CHAPTER 11

■■■■■■■■

WHAT KEY SCIENTISTS HAVE TO SAY

MIAMI: PREPARING FOR NEW RESEARCH

● ●

I *had been home for about a month,* reading and analyzing the material I'd gathered, before I realized that there were areas I still wanted to explore personally before I started to write.

The anthropology of the shroud images, for example, had been delved into by few researchers—Luigi Gedda and Giulio Ricci were the only two names that came to mind. They had gone to great lengths to measure the different parts of the body as delineated in the shroud, but they had said little about what racial characteristics the figure revealed.

To get an objective, impartial analysis of my own, I telephoned the Smithsonian National Museum of Natural Sciences in Washington, D.C., and asked to speak to an anthropologist.

T. Dale Stewart picked up the phone; he had been director of the museum between 1962 and 1965 and was now anthropologist emeritus.

When I explained to him what I wanted, he said that although he had never heard of the shroud, it did sound interesting. He said also that he would be happy to meet with me, but asked that I first send him some material on the shroud, especially the Enrie photos.

I could see a trip to Washington looming.

For further information on the textile aspects of the shroud, I decided to write again to the two museums in Lyons, the ones Pére Bourguet had suggested I visit to see if I could find among the pieces of the Gayet collection facial or bodily imprints on the burial clothes found in Antione, Egypt. In re-checking Vignon's 1902 book on the shroud, I came across this startling paragraph:

M. Gayet has shown me all sorts of shrouds found in Egyptian tombs. In some cases, the mummy has left vague imprints on the enveloping cloth like a brown stain devoid of shape and gradation. I have thought I recognized the print of a back, but no distinct shape was visible. M. Gayet was good enough to give me the Egyptian shroud on which this brown shading was perceptible. Perhaps some day it may serve to prove that there is no resemblance between the mark on this coarse outer casing and the print at Turin, which is equivalent to a portrait. There is no possible resemblance between the stains caused by...decomposition and the picture produced [on the shroud].

So it seems that Vignon had not only met Gayet, but had also come to the same conclusion as I—albeit some seventy years before my trip to the Louvre. While I'd keep alert for shrouds or veils with distinguishable body imprints, perhaps it was best to spend more time and resources on other aspects of the story.

■■■■■■■■

Another area I felt had not been sufficiently explored was Jewish burial practices. I telephoned the Jewish Theological Seminary in New York City, explained my problem to the public relations office, and was connected to Dr. Dov Zlotnic, professor of rabbinic literature. Intrigued by my question, but unable to discuss the several possible answers by telephone, Dr. Zlotnic said that he would see me any time during my next visit to Manhattan.

The reason I telephoned Jewish Theological was that Father Edward Wuenschel had also met with someone there. He was one of the few sindonologists who actually consulted Jewish experts for information on ancient Jewish burial procedures. In the foreword to his book about the shroud, *Self-Portrait of Christ*, he acknowledged "special thanks to Rabbi Jacob Menkes, a noted authority on rabbinical lore."

■■■■■■■■

In searching for the most probable theory of how the images were actually transferred to the cloth, I decided to try the young science of parapsychology, which dealt with strange and unusual phenomena. I telephoned Dr. Karlis Osis, head of the American Society for Psychical Research in New York City.

Osis said he would be glad to see me, but didn't I think that an optical physicist would be the appropriate person to study the shroud photographs? The one he recommended was Dr. John Rush, professor at the University of Colorado, Boulder.

The reason I particularly wanted to meet with Osis was that he had conducted an interesting study in which he had questioned approximately 640 doctors and nurses who attended deathbed patients. The results were dramatic. A significant number of the medical professionals reported that the dying patients were in "an elevated mood" just before their deaths, speaking of a kind of otherworld which they seemed to be moving into; they even got angry when some of the doctors tried to revive them. "It's so beautiful there," the moribund had said. Were they getting glimpses of what the shroud may be showing—resurrection? As improbable as that sounded, the shroud itself was improbable. I wanted to hear about it.

■■■■■■■■

Still another area I felt needed exploration was photographic analysis. Remembering I had once seen a magazine that mentioned a Kodak man in connection with the shroud, I dug through my mountain of shroud material until I found it: a letter to the editor of the *British Journal of Photography*, dated June 30, 1967.

Walter Clark was the letter-writer's name. He wrote that he was affiliated with Eastman Kodak Company's research laboratories, and that in 1930 or 1931 a Lieutenant Colonel P. W. O'Gorman had come from England to ask him some questions about the shroud image. Clark said he had volunteered a guess: peroxides from the burial spices had caused oxidation of the linen, and this in turn formed an image. Ammonias, in a process called chemical vapography, were known to do this on cellulose, and linen, he pointed out, was cellulose. In other words, as Clark saw it, the shroud image was the result of chemical vapography, but through peroxide vapors instead of ammonia vapors, and without a sensitized cloth.

I decided to try a long shot. I called telephone information in Rochester and got a number. Much to my surprise and delight, Clark answered the phone. We talked awhile, but Clark said there wasn't anything he could add to the explanation he'd offered forty years before. The trouble with that explanation, I told him, was that some chemists don't believe vapors will travel in straight lines and thus etch a good image. Clark maintained (like Vignon before him) that they might be able to do so if the atmosphere were still and damp enough.

He added that O'Gorman hadn't liked the straight chemical explanation either.

The article that O'Gorman wrote on the shroud appeared in the May 1931 issue of *The Catholic Medical Guardian*. He later revised and expanded his theory into a speech which he gave in London; the speech appeared in a 1940 issue of the *American Ecclesiastical Review*.

What O'Gorman came up with was a theory combining the action of four different agents: oxidizing vapors such as those postulated by Vignon, radioactive substances which may have been in the burial spices or even in the body parts themselves, "electrical radiations of an auracal nature," and "a sudden radiance of our Lord's body at the moment of the resurrection."

The best thing for me to do now, Clark suggested, was to contact Charles Bridgeman at the Kodak Marketing Educational Center in Rochester. "He has vast experience in the examination of works of art and in the techniques of radiography, ultraviolet light, and infrared photography, and I think he'd be the best one able to pass judgment on the new shroud photos."

I thanked Clark and took his advice. I called Bridgeman, who said he'd be glad to look at the photos if I would just send them up.

Several weeks later I got his response:

What an exciting thrill it was to see the photographs of the shroud of Turin. The more one studies these pictures, the clearer it becomes that any evaluation based upon them alone would be of little help unless a thorough scientific examination were undertaken, and this seems out of the question.

My specific area of investigation involves radiography, and even in this area, I could not state what created a specific image on the film without a chemical analysis of the substance traversed by the X-rays. I hope you can see that any comment I might make would be of no value.

Radiation was an intriguing theory, and I decided to telephone the University of Miami Medical School, where I was given the name of Dr. Harold E. Davis, a retired professor of radiology and a fellow of the American College of Radiology.

He lived not far from me. When I showed him the Enrie photographs, he remarked that they resembled X-rays; beyond that he was unwilling to comment. For an expert opinion, he suggested I consult someone else, like E. Dale Trout of the University of Oregon, who, he said, had been one of General Electric's finest radiation physicists.

Trout, when I reached him by phone, suggested that the one to see was Wade Patterson, a radiation physicist at the Lawrence Livermore Laboratory near San Francisco, a facility run by the University of California at Berkeley for the U.S. Atomic Energy Commission.

Patterson said he would be glad to receive me, and we made an appointment.

THE NUCLEAR CONNECTION

Since it appeared I would be spending some time in the very near future in California, I decided to try to track down Ralph Graeber, sometimes called "the guy with the shroud show" in

Southern California. It turned out, when I finally got him on the phone, that he had not only undergone a sort of religious conversion, but that he was also a nuclear engineer. The profile of him that evolved in the next few days from telephone calls and letters made him as intriguing and as potentially important to the shroud story as Hans Naber and Leonard Cheshire.

After World War II, during which he served as a B-25 pilot, Graeber enrolled at Purdue University. As a student of engineering, he worked part time on the university's nuclear project, which was the development of a "linear electron accelerator and synchrotron," more commonly known as an atom smasher. After graduation he took a job with the U.S. Atomic Energy Commission's Argonne National Laboratory located at Lemont, Illinois; there he helped develop two of the first big "Van Neumann class" scientific computers, the AVIDAC and the ORACLE.

In 1953, partly because of his work on the pioneering science computers, Graeber was asked to join RCA's budding missile project at Cape Canaveral, Florida. RCA's contract called for the processing of missile flight-test data, and Graeber was asked to work with the team building two SEAC-class computers that were to do the job. When ballistic missiles with supersonic thrusts were fired down the Atlantic Testing Range, he was responsible for one of the first "online" computers. And he was at Canaveral when the first American satellites went up.

During this time of rich scientific fulfillment, however, Graeber underwent strong religious disillusionment. "As a scientist, I gradually began to realize that theologians and ministers didn't know what they were talking about. Time and again they would spew scientific errors from the pulpit till I couldn't stand Sunday morning church anymore. This understanding coalesced in the late 1950s while I was at Canaveral. Yet I felt inside that the basic Bible must contain truth, and that the fault therefore lay with its self-appointed interpreters."

So he started looking through "the occult stuff" and found most of it nauseating, except perhaps the writings of Edgar Cayce and Emmanuel Swedenborg, both of whom were psychics, the one twentieth-century American, the other eighteenth-century Swedish.

Then Graeber read *Autobiography of a Yogi*, a 1946 metaphysical work by the Indian spiritual master Parmahansa Yogananda. "I found the autobiography by far the best philosophy-of-life book that I had ever encountered," Graeber told me. "I was totally captivated by its profound scientific insights. And I was even more impressed that these insights could be used to remove blockages that inhibit man from using his psychic and intuitional powers. But I also was not naïve, and I knew that Southern California [where Yogananda's followers, the Self-Realization Fellowship, had established its headquarters] was full of kooks. So I prayed very hard to Jesus to tell me if Yogananda's message was the same that Jesus had taught. Then, the very next issue of the *Self-Realization* magazine had the shroud face printed on the rear cover, and the instant I saw it I realized fully that it was the answer to my prayer."

The expression on the shroud face was exactly like the expression Graeber had seen so many times on pictures of Yogananda's face, he said, and in many respects like the expression on the face of Yogananda's master, Sri Yukteswar, who died in 1935.

"It is said that a picture is worth ten thousand words," Graeber said, "and to me the similarities were a positive and total indication that both Yogananda and Jesus knew and taught the same things."

Graeber left Canaveral in the early 1960s and took a job in Burbank, California, where he could be near the Self-Realization centers. "I still had a great love for Jesus and his teachings, and I considered it pitiful that his millions of followers knew nothing of the true photograph of him and the deep insight into his nature which it conveyed." So, seeing the shroud as a vehicle that might bring about this enlightenment, and also seeing that his scientific background was uniquely suited to spread the shroud story, Graeber said that, along with learning from Yogananda, he would become unofficial publicity man for the shroud on the West Coast.

His first project was to assemble a slide show. For pictures, he said, he sent away to the Holy Shroud Guild in Esopus, New York. For specific information, he read books by Wuenschel and Barbet. Then he took to the road, showing the slides all over Southern California.

Next, Graeber decided to design and sell shroud greeting cards. His first was a simple one: the shroud face on one side, and on the other, a poem he'd written about the relic. The second card was more sophisticated; on the front it displayed one of the beautiful NASA photographs of earth as seen from outer space, with the word "peace" superimposed; on the inside was a picture of the positive shroud face, with considerable text explaining the shroud images on the slides Graeber showed. "The text was very heavy," said Graeber. "It was a mixture of Eastern philosophy and Western science, and the groundswell of interest I had envisioned never developed."

After Graeber and I had spoken long distance a couple times, I began to realize that he felt the images on the shroud had been formed by some kind of radiation from the body, and that the radiation had possibly caused heat. "To space-age scientists, it is quite obvious that images were formed by radiation processes," said a paragraph in the text on one of his cards. "And the linen was scorched by the Nova," said a line in the poem on the other.

Graeber's use of the word "scorched" made me rifle through the notes I had taken in Turin. In a few moments I found what I was looking for. Yes, Father Peter Rinaldi had used the same word to describe the body imprints the day he and I saw the shroud in the Hall of the Swiss.

Both Graeber and Rinaldi describing the shroud images as being scorched onto the linen reminded me of an article I had read in a 1966 issue of *Sindon*, the journal of the Cultores Sanctae Sindonis in Turin. The author of the article was British journalist and writer Geoffrey Ashe. His theory was that the images on the shroud may have been the result of scorching. To test his theory, he took a horse brass, which is a metal medallion about three inches in diameter with a horse in relief in its center. He heated the medallion, placed it relief-side-up on a flat surface, and then laid a handkerchief over it, stretching the handkerchief gently "so as to smooth it out and give as uniform a contact as possible without direct pressure or sagging."

After a few seconds, Ashe wrote that "a brown 'scorch-picture' was visibly forming and coming through to the upper side." He quickly lifted the cloth from the metal, and the result was a very detailed, negative picture of the horse. All the parts of the figure that were in direct contact with the handkerchief came out dark; the parts not in direct contact came out lighter or not at all. Ashe concluded:

> The physical change of the body at the resurrection may have released a brief and violent burst of some radiation other than heat—perhaps scientifically identifiable, perhaps not—which scorched the cloth. In this case, the shroud is a quasi-photograph of Christ returning to life, produced by a kind of radiance or "incandescence" partially analogous to heat in its effects. . . . In conclusion, the acceptance of the holy shroud as a "scorch picture"—whatever the precise mode of creation—justifies the following statement: "The shroud is explicable [only] if it once

enwrapped a human body to which something extraordinary happened. It is not explicable otherwise."

The flash-of-heat-and-light theory advanced by O'Gorman in the 1930s and Ashe in the 1960s seemed to be acquiring a new respectability in the 1970s.

"The one thing you must realize," Graeber said to me, "is that man's body is not what it appears to be. This is basic to nuclear science, space-age science, and occult science. The body is a marvelous collection of spinning electrons grouped into cells, and these cells are grouped into nerves, blood, muscle, bone, et cetera. And all the time there is continuous electrical motion in the atoms, and where there is electrical motion there are electromagnetic fields, and electromagnetic fields radiate out....In a nutshell, the radiations are there whether anybody wants to say they are or not. They always have been, and always will be, wherever matter exists."

I knew in a general way what Graeber was talking about. While doing research in parapsychology for articles I'd written, I had come across scientists who, in arguing for the existence of immaterial entities such as a surviving consciousness after death, had pointed out that matter, contrary to the way it appears to the human senses, is not, at its essence, material.

They had explained it this way:

All things are made of atoms, and atoms are made of protons, neutrons, electrons, and other atomic particles. But none of these particles are matter in the same way that a table or a chair is. They are described as being made out of "electricity" or "energy." Some parts of the atom actually exhibit the characteristics of "antimatter," a word coined to express their essential immateriality. These are strange particles, and their very existence means that there is a basic non-materiality in all material things.

Einstein's famous formula—energy equals mass times the velocity of light squared—was an expression of this basic immateriality. It stated that material, or mass, is nothing more than converted energy, and that energy is nothing but converted mass. But what is energy? Although scientists could name its various forms—heat, light, electricity, and so forth—no one really knew.

Now, in relation to the shroud, Graeber was expanding my knowledge of nuclear science when he explained that the moving electron—one of the mysterious parts of the atom—gives off radiation. And since all things are made of atoms, it therefore follows that all things give off radiation.

"Man is not the 150-pound chunk of solid matter portrayed by the very limited five senses," iterated Graeber. "He never was, and never will be. Man is 'in the image of God'—spinning constantly, changing cycles, from the tiniest electrons to the entire body. And the electrons circling their centers are surely 'in the image' of earths circling suns, suns circling galaxies, and galaxies circling what scientists now call the 'big bang' center, which yogis in the ancient Vedas had long called 'Vishnuave.'"

Graeber, much as it sounded, said he wasn't trying to be mystical.

"It is wrong to refer to the radiation that caused the shroud images as extra-natural. Its operation is the operation of a natural law that stuffed-shirt Western science simply hasn't gotten around to investigating. . . . The Greeks gave us the concept of the atom thousands of years before the West ever got around to its so-called discovery. The masses consider natural that which is *familiar*—not that which is explained. The human heartbeat is much more extra-natural than the shroud image, but it is considered natural only because it is so familiar. And it will probably be a long time before the shroud radiation becomes equally familiar.

"All discovery of new scientific laws starts with a flash of mental insight into the causative elements of a perplexing situation. Then comes the publishing of the new concept; the entrenched-position people then heap fire on the head of the innovator, controversy flourishes, and eventually a majority BECOME AWARE of the new idea, and judge it to be true. Thus the concept becomes a scientific law until a new and better—deeper and more comprehensive—concept comes along. The scientific awareness of radiation basically only dates back to World War II.

"And there is also the matter of degrees of explanations to be kept in mind when talking of the shroud images. Nothing is ever fully explained. When a phenomenon is reproducible, that which is enough to satisfy a majority of observers changes constantly. For example, prior to photography, the image was explained as a miracle, and this satisfied the masses. So it was considered explained. After photography, there was the vapography, which, for a while, was accepted as the explanation—and it did crudely reproduce the negative phenomenon. Now radiation must be added, and it too will serve for a while. Then other things will be found, and it will be explained again and again—and so on.

"I really don't know if we'll ever be able to fully comprehend what happened in the shroud—at least not until our understandings are raised to the highest level."

■■■■■■■■■

Before leaving for Washington, D.C., I decided to write to the European sindonologists I'd met to inquire if anyone had consulted a nuclear physicist on the possibility of radiation causing the images on the shroud.

I also sent a letter to the U.S. Department of Commerce's National Technical Information Service and the *Encyclopaedia*

Britannica's research service. Any mentions of the images of human corpses being transferred to cloths would be most appreciated, I wrote, and I enclosed checks to cover their fees.

They were very sorry, both organizations wrote back, but to their knowledge no such references existed, unless one counts those mentions of the shroud of Turin from the fourteenth century on.

CHAPTER 12

■■■■■■■■

MORE FROM THE EXPERTS

ORIGINS OF THE MAN IN THE SHROUD

● ● ● ● ● ● ● ● ● ● ● ● ● ● ● ● ● ● ● ●

W*hen I arrived at the Smithsonian* National Museum of Natural Sciences, I was greeted in the north foyer by a sabor-toothed tiger. The sign said it was a pre-historic beast, but the taxidermist had made it look as though it was about to devour me for its lunch.

I asked for T. Dale Stewart and was told he had gone for a bite to eat. Once again I had to wait.

While waiting, I had a chance to reread the conclusion of *The Shroud of Turin* by the German Jesuit Werner Bulst. The book had been published in Germany in 1954 and in the United States in 1956.

Bulst had this to say about the man in the shroud's origins:

Is it possible to determine more closely the nationality of this man on the cloth? Since we have only a frontal image, and moreover, since the color of the skin, hair, and eyes is unknown, it would hardly seem possible to directly determine the racial strain with certitude. Still, the style of wearing the hair and beard allows some deductions. The man was certainly not of the Greco-Roman culture. Of the numerous portraits we have of Greek and Roman origin, there is not one of a man with hair parted in the middle and falling to the shoulders. Likewise, a beard like that which appears on the cloth of Turin is seldom found. Is this in keeping with a Jew in the time of Christ? There was hardly a people in the whole Roman Empire who clung so stubbornly to their customs which, for the most part, were determined by their religious beliefs. It is well known that, in contrast to other peoples, the Jews highly regarded the beard as a manly adornment.

However, we do not know exactly how men wore their hair in the time of Jesus. But, again in contrast with other peoples even neighboring on Israel, longish hair was thoroughly in keeping with Jewry. In his researches into the Jewish style of wearing the hair, H. Grossman found that they generally wore long hair caught together at the back of the neck. S. Kraus, the distinguished Jewish archaeologist, maintains that both in the Talmudic and biblical period to which Grossman extended his study, men wore "long hair" but "not too long"—a flexible gauge.

In any case we can say that the "portrait" on the cloth of Turin agrees perfectly with what we know from other sources of the Jewish style of wearing the hair. Still, these scraps of information are too meager to allow any conclusive proof.

Stewart was a leading anthropologist. I hoped that my meeting with him could shed more light on this question of the origins of the man in the shroud.

■■■■■■■■

Once Stewart arrived back from lunch, we walked through some of the halls of the institution to his office. I saw the packet of shroud information on his desk, but it turned out that he hadn't had a chance to look at it. He was attentive to my story, however, and when I finished, he made some comments.

"The effect is of a narrow face, characteristic of the Caucasoid people—a white man. Orientals tend to be round-faced. Negroes have broad noses and thick lips. That means he could be Semitic, but I would have to see the profile to tell for sure. It looks like a large nose, and it might have been quite prominent. But there's no way to be certain without a profile."

If I had known Stewart would need a profile of the man in the shroud, I would have brought along the photographs made by Leo Vala, a photographer of British royalty and a pioneer in the development of the 3-D visual process and cinemascope movie screens. By manipulating light through photo transparencies, he produced an image on a normal screen that enabled sculptors to make a three-dimensional model, which could then be photographed in profile or indeed from any other angle. In perfecting the process, Vala had selected the shroud face as a subject "because," Vala said, "it's such a beautiful image."

After publishing the results of his experimentation in the March 8, 1967, issue of *Amateur Photographer*, Vala became an outspoken critic of anyone who thought the image could have been produced by human hands either through artistry or technology. "I've been involved in the invention of many complicated visual processes, and I can tell you that no one could have faked that image. No one could do it today with all the technology we have. It's a perfect negative. It has a photographic quality that is extremely precise."

The more scholarly *British Journal of Photography* published an article on the cloth soon after, and it provoked considerable comment—both pro and con—from its readership.

Stewart, at least, as we talked in his office, was narrowing the questions: "But this comes so close to the traditional representation of Christ," Stewart went on to say, "that you have a built-in bias to contend with. However, that also raises the question of whether artists could have been following some model"—as Vignon had posed with his iconographic theory.

The reason Vignon had developed the iconographic theory was that he was a painter—and, as it turned out, so too was Stewart in his leisure time.

The FBI, said Stewart, frequently asked him to identify the race of a person by bones that agents would bring in, but obviously I could not provide bones in this case.

Blood Type

Although this has never been absolutely confirmed, certain tests have indicated that the blood on the shroud is type AB.

"We can't go beyond broad racial stocks with so little evidence," Stewart said. "We can say these are from a white man, a Negro, or a Mongoloid. But you really need to see a person in life to be positive. The shroud face is that of a white man. I think we can say that. But whether he was from Palestine or Greece, I don't know. I don't think you can be that specific. You'd be challenged. People would say, 'How do you know? What's your proof?'"

Stewart suggested that I put the question to Carlton S. Coon, one of the world's most distinguished ethnologists. A former Harvard professor and ethnology curator at the University of Pennsylvania, Coon, who also had served as an OSS agent (forerunner of the CIA) in World War II, had written books on the racial classifications of people all over the world. "He'd be the man who might be able to give you some answers," Stewart told me.

Following Stewart's advice, I wrote to Coon, who had requested photos of the shroud from me when I'd reached him by phone.

"Here are the pictures you asked me to return," Coon later wrote back. "Whoever the individual represented may have been, he is of a physical type found in modern times among Sephardic Jews and noble Arabs. The soft parts of the nose have shrunken a bit, which is simply a sign of death. I have seen the same thing in the mummies of Egyptian pharaohs.

"For what it is worth, that is my opinion."

Coon's opinion was worth a great deal, especially in view of the fact that he had traveled widely throughout the Middle East, Asia, South America, and Africa. He was also the author of fifteen books in the area of anthropology, including *The Origin of Races*, published in 1962, and *The Living Races of Man*, published in 1965. As if these weren't enough accreditation, he is credited with the discovery of at least one ancient-man fossil, Arterian man, and with leading the expeditions that discovered two others: Hotu man and Jebel Ighoud man No. 2.

MORE TEXTILE RESEARCH

My next stop in Washington was the Textile Museum on S Street where I hoped to show the shroud photographs to a staff expert.

When I had written my first set of articles on the shroud in 1971, I called the museum from Miami to find out if linen cloth could have survived two thousand years.

Anthony Landreau, the acting director at that time, said there was no doubt that it could. "We have fragments of linen preserved from 10,000 BC," he said.

Arriving at the museum's reception room, I was referred to a young woman assistant; when I told her what I wanted, she looked most skeptical indeed. She said there was no one available at the moment, but if I wanted to leave the photographs with a note, she would see to it that they reached someone who knew about such things; nothing, however, could be done that day. She probably thought I was some kind of religious fanatic. As I headed for the door, I knew I would not be hearing from the Textile Museum any time in the near future.

Some time later Louise Mackie, associate curator of the Textile Museum, told me over the phone that she didn't believe any conclusive statements could be made about the shroud on the basis of photographs alone. "Seeing and handling make a difference," she said. "However, it appears to be a very basic weave. Maybe someone with experience in Middle Eastern fabrics could tell you more." She suggested a curator at the Metropolitan Museum in New York, but I was never able to make the connection.

HIROSHIMA

· · · · · · · · · · · · · · · · ·

Ever since seeing them in a book, I had been intrigued by the strange shadow-silhouettes formed on Hiroshima walls at the moment the atomic bomb was detonated above that city in 1945. A flash of heat or light—or both—was said to have caused them. The same—or probably a lesser degree of the same—might have been involved in forming the shroud images. My visit to Turin had shown the shroud images resembled scorch marks.

Tracking down the possibilities that the Hiroshima images might be related to those on the shroud, I visited the library of D.C.'s Atomic Energy Commission. There I located several books, one of which was a 1972 work entitled *The Day Man Lost*. Authorship was ascribed to a group called the Pacific War Research Society, and the publisher was Kodansha International, Ltd., of Tokyo, Japan, and Palo Alto, California. Photographs of some of the shadows were included in the book. One showed the shadow of a ladder that had once been permanently attached to a watertank; another, the rough silhouette of a man who had been sitting on stone steps. But the book was not clear as to exactly how the strange images had been formed. On returning to the hotel, I wrote for more information to the Hiroshima Peace Memorial Museum.

"We received your letter inquiring about shadows formed at the time of the A-bomb blast in our city," wrote back Kazuharu Hemasaki, curator of the Hiroshima Peace Memorial Museum.

Frankly speaking, we have no definite idea whether the shadows were formed only by heat rays or gamma rays, or by both heat rays and gamma rays. But here in Hiroshima, it is widely believed that the shadows were made by enormous heat rays burning or melting everything. And when the heat rays were blocked by objects in their path, unburned areas were made right behind the objects as shadows of them.

Obviously, no atom bomb blast had caused the images on the shroud. The linen wouldn't exist if it had. But, as Graber had explained, the human body is, at its essence, a mass of swirling atoms and atom parts. The shroud, no matter what one believes, conjures resurrection. How, if there was a resurrection, could it have happened? Dematerialization of the body into whatever it became in spirit life was, as far as current hardcore science was concerned, fiction. But if that's what had happened in the cloth, as Christians believe, there might have been a release of heat or light or both, albeit much less than what occurred at Hiroshima. Such rays might have etched parts of the shroud image not in contact with the cloth. But I'd struck out on this line of inquiry and had to put it to rest.

■■■■■■■■

Since the shroud seemed to be the bloody remnant of an execution, I decided to try another long shot. I telephoned the FBI and asked if someone in their crime lab could look at the Enrie photographs and attempt an analysis of the causes of death.

I was told to send the material and to await a response that would definitely be forthcoming.

"Our normal policy," replied Clarence M. Kelley, newly appointed director of the FBI,

> requires that the FBI laboratory conduct examinations of evidence in criminal cases for all duly constituted law enforcement agencies. Although exceptions to this policy are possible, it has been found that examinations of the type you requested from photographs are not productive. Examination of the original material would be a more appropriate procedure; however, since such material is in custody of another country, it is not within the province of this Bureau to conduct such examinations.

■■■■■■■■

MYSTERIOUS LEAVES, GHOSTLY PHOTOS

DR. ROBERT BUCKLIN

. . . .

My *first stop in California* was San Diego, the new home of Dr. Robert Bucklin. He was the Midwestern clinical pathologist who had written an article on the shroud which appeared in the January 1970 issue of *Medicine, Science, and the Law*, a journal of the British Academy of Sciences. He helped me in some of the medical areas pertaining to the relic, including making a determination about Hans Naber's several theories; he didn't think they were accurate.

RALPH GRAEBER

• •

The next day I flew to Los Angeles. Ralph Graeber's voice on the telephone had suggested a suntanned, military-looking technician like the type often seen in NASA photographs. I was surprised, then, when a tall, thin, conservatively dressed gentleman of about fifty walked forward and unassumingly introduced himself as the engineer with whom I'd been corresponding.

He told me that after a series of personal and financial troubles, two good things had happened. He had gotten together many of his ideas on modern science and religion, and he was offered a job on the research staff of Systems Development Corporation, a division of the Rand Corporation, the think-tank company used frequently by the American government.

With the help of the sophisticated computers at SDC, he hoped to initiate a new shroud project: restoration of the shroud images to an almost flawless state by using "space-age image-correction techniques." These techniques had been developed by NASA's Jet Propulsion Lab to correct lens distortion and other "noise" in photographs taken by unmanned space probes. The result would be a sharper, more detailed shroud face.

Once in the car together and settled into a lane on the freeway, Graeber began responding to my questions about the probable origin of the images on the shroud.

It was obvious to any space-age scientist, he said, that the images could have been produced only by some kind of wavelength radiation—by what might commonly be called rays. Vapors don't travel in straight lines, but radiation does. He didn't know precisely what kind of radiation it was, but he told me he felt sure that it was the same kind involved in the formation of the Volckringer leaves.

He was referring to the experiments in image transfer done by Dr. Jean Volckringer during the 1940s. Rummaging through old herbals and plant books with specimens pressed inside, Dr. Volckringer, chief apothecary at St. Joseph's Hospital, Paris, noticed that sometimes a nearly identical image of a leaf would be formed several pages away from the one on which it was mounted. Somehow, the specimen had projected or radiated its image through the pages covering it and onto a blank page beyond. The resulting images were not only sharp—as photographs of them testify—but they were also negatives. They were approximately the same color as the shroud stains—brown—and they even appeared to fade imperceptibly as the shroud stains clearly do. These images were "like a design in sepia," Volckringer was quoted as saying in Barbet's *Doctor at Calvary*.

"None of these images were to be found in recent herbals," remarked Barbet in *Doctor at Calvary*. "They were, for instance, very clear in an herbal of 1836, while there were scarcely any markings in an herbal of 1908, which at the time [when Volckringer discovered them] made them 34 years old."

If it had taken a century for the herbals to project or radiate their images, it is no wonder that sindonologists did not consider radiation a possible explanation for the images on the shroud; after all, as the absence of decomposition stains indicates, the man had been in the shroud for only a few short hours.

In the same breath as the Volckringer leaves, Graeber mentioned Kirlian photography as a type of radiation possibly involved in the formation of images on the shroud.

In 1939, Semyon Kirlian, a Soviet electrician, while observing a demonstration of a high-frequency machine being used in electrotherapy, noticed a tiny flash of light between the electrodes attached to the patient and the patient's skin. Curious, he wondered if he could photograph it, and accordingly he built himself a high-frequency machine at home. He created a high-frequency electronic field between an electrode from the machine and a metal plate, inserted a piece of film between the two, and placed his hand on the film. Though Kirlian got a severe burn for his efforts, he also got a brilliant photograph of his hand, with a luminescence, or halo, or aura, along the contours of the fingers.

After refining his machine, he began photographing all sorts of objects, dead and alive—things such as leaves, coins, and fingers. Eventually, with still further refinements, he was able to photograph entire human bodies without the intermediary of film. And always the results were the same: a glowing luminescence that seemed to radiate from the subject in a myriad of hues—red, blue, green, yellow, and white—rising, fluctuating, churning.

"Around the edges of a leaf," wrote Sheila Otrander and Lynn Schroeder in *Psychic Discoveries Behind the Iron Curtain*,

> there were turquoise and reddish-yellow patterns of flares coming out of specific channels.... A human finger placed in the high-frequency field...showed up like a complex topographical map. There were lines, points, craters of lights, and flares. Some parts of the finger looked like a carved jack-o'-lantern with a glowing light inside.... [The hand] looked like the Milky Way in a starry sky....Multicolored flares lit up, then sparks, twinkles, flashes. Some lights glowed steadily like Roman candles; others flashed out, then dimmed. Still others sparked at intervals.

But what was the luminescence? What was Kirlian seeing? No one knew for sure, wrote Ostrander and Schroeder, but after years of observation, Soviet scientists called it "bio-radiation" or an "energy body" that was somehow inside and emanating from all things.

In living things, the emanations appeared to be connected with health. When the aura looked dim and lacking in vibrancy, the person being photographed was found to be either already sick or on his or her way to becoming sick. When it looked strong and brilliant, the person was well and feeling good. The aura wasn't restricted to physical health alone. Anger, hate, tenderness, and joy showed up markedly in the photographs and through the viewing machine. An angry person's aura, for example, turned bright red; blue was a sign of tranquility.

In dead things, the aura seemed to be the slowly diminishing "essence of life." But since completely lifeless things such as coins also had a luminescence, some scientists were moved to speculate that this was the "skeleton" of what had once had life. Unlike the "energy-body" of live things, the luminescence of metals was pure white, completely colorless.

One of the most surprising finds, according to the American researchers, was that when the Soviet scientists cut part of a subject away—for instance, part of a leaf—they would still get an aura from the section that was missing and in exactly the same shape as the missing part. In other words, the "energy-body" still showed where the material body had been cut off.

Is this the reason why amputees sometimes say that they still feel their severed limb or have sensations in that limb? Ostrander and Schroeder didn't conclude one way or the other, but it was hypothesized from their account of Kirlian photography that the human body had been discovered to emit radiation.

The only difference between the Volckringer leaves and the Kirlian images was a matter of degree, Graeber said as we continued along the freeway. "The more evolved the matter—from mineral to vegetable, to animal, to man, to saint, and so on—the greater the amplitude of radiation." So great saints, or those of the 'I-am' consciousness, he said, are surrounded by powerful auras, or halos.

"Jesus and saints of all religions have always been portrayed with halos around them. The reason for this is that their radiations were so intense that they could be seen with the naked eye."

The naked eye of the apostles maybe, I thought, or of some other enlightened individuals. I myself had never seen an aura, although I can't say others had not. Graeber's statement reminded me of the gospel account of the transfiguration, during which Peter, James, and John saw Jesus radiating a brilliant light. Theologians have speculated that the apostles were actually allowed a glimpse of Jesus' divinity in this moment.

Graeber continued: "The Volckringer leaves, however, gave off such low-intensity radiation that it was—what was it?—a hundred years, I believe, after the herbals had been on the shelves before anyone discovered the images."

The Transfiguration: An Aura?

And after six days Jesus took with him Peter and James and John, and led them up a high mountain apart by themselves; and he was transfigured before them, and his garments became glistening, intensely white, as no fuller on earth could bleach them.

—Mark 9:2–3

"But why," it seemed a natural question to ask, "had Jesus' radiation been strong enough to make marks on the cloth of the shroud, when none of the other bodies that had been put in shrouds ever had?"

"Kirlian photography shows that both mental and physical stress increase the loss of life-energy from the body. Now Jesus suffered both extreme mental anguish and extreme physical torture—as much as any man I've ever heard of—before his death. Thus, the intensity level of radiation from his body would have been very great in the tomb."

Besides, Jesus was the very embodiment of the highest consciousness there is, added Graeber: the "Son of God" consciousness. Therefore, his aura was stronger than any other.

There was still another reason why the images in Volckringer's herbals might resemble the shroud images so much. Both the linen of the shroud and the high-grade paper on which the herbals were presumably printed were made of the same vegetable compound, cellulose. Consequently, the Volckringer-Kirlian radiation would have produced approximately the same softly diffused brown stain on the molecular structures of the cellulose material.

The crucial differences between the two types of radiation are in the variables of intensity, exposure duration, and possibly development time. "The Volckringer images were produced by a low-intensity exposure over a long period of time," Graeber said, "and the shroud images were produced by a high-intensity exposure over a short period of time. And we don't really know what the development times of either were."

To further prove that a little-known radiation emanates from the body, Graeber gave me the address of a San Francisco man who, he said, was able to see auras with the naked eye. And Graeber promised to give me a copy of a paraphyschological classic entitled *The Aura* by J. W. Kilner, a late nineteenth-century physician at St. Thomas's Hospital, London. Kilner, aware of the claims of persons who said they could see the aura with the unaided eye, invented an optical device through which he said he could see the aura himself.

■ ■ ■ ■ ■ ■ ■

After dinner, Graeber invited me to see the space observatory in Griffith Park, a preserve atop the mountains high above the city from which the Pacific Ocean beyond could be seen—a fitting place in the twinkling evening for our spiritual discussion.

I asked him to speculate on exactly what kind of radiation the Volckringer-Kirlian radiation might be.

"Anything I say in this area would be un-provable in terms of volumes of formalized proofs," he said reluctantly. "But I suspect it is somewhere in the ultraviolet region of electromagnetic radiation."

Ultraviolet radiation was close to visible light, I knew, and there it would be a good candidate for what "sensitives" were actually perceiving when they reported seeing the human aura. Ultraviolet rays could burn, given enough intensity, and therefore they could have caused the scorched look that the shroud images seem to have.

Graeber didn't like my characterizing the shroud images as "scorched." He'd come to prefer to say that the mysterious radiation had acted on the shroud in a manner somewhat analogous to heat, but without heat's harshness. The action, he thought, was perhaps more like light on a photographic plate.

Before I left Los Angeles, Graeber and I would see each other several more times, and we would cover the same ground again. Later he sent me a copy of *The Kirlian Aura*, by Stanley Krippner and Daniel Rubin. Thinking about Graeber, I decided he was an exemplary member of a growing number of scientists who were moving away from hardcore materialism.

CHAPTER 14

■■■■■■■■

SPACE-AGE SCIENCE

THE CARBON 14 TEST

. . . .

My next stop was UCLA to show the shroud photographs to Dr. Willard Libby, a chemist and expert in Carbon 14 dating, a fairly new scientific method for determining the ages of ancient specimens which sindonologists hoped might someday be used on the shroud. Libby had been awarded all sorts of honors and prizes—including a Nobel Prize—for his work in organic and nuclear chemistry.

With the aid of large machines called counters, scientists can determine—usually, but not always with a great deal of accuracy—the amount of Carbon 14 left in an object, and from that data they compute the object's age. By taking two pieces of the linen that wrapped some of the Dead Sea Scrolls, Libby had been able to date the ancient parchments back to just before the time of Christ—around 100 BC or so, with an accuracy of plus-or-minus fifty years.

The entire subject itself was interesting:

For the past 50,000 years, all living things have absorbed just about the same amount of Carbon 14, an atom that originates in the atmosphere and is then absorbed by plants and animals. Once the plant or animal dies, this fixed amount of Carbon 14 begins to disintegrate at a fixed rate, which is approximately 50 percent of itself every 5,730 years. In other words, every 5,730 years, the amount of Carbon 14 in the remains of the dead plant or animal is approximately half of what it was 5,730 years before.

Regarding the shroud, a Carbon 14 test had already been proposed by, among others, Walter C. McCrone Associates, Inc., of Chicago. No more than one-sixth of an ounce of the linen would be consumed, said the company. The McCrone Lab had recently analyzed the "Vinland Map" for Yale University and declared the claimed early fifteenth-century cartographic rendering of America to be a fake. (This is a contention that is still being debated.) The cost of the test as of 1977 would have been $12,500, an amount that American sindonologists were more than willing to subsidize.

In my meeting with Dr. Libby, a very busy man, I outlined the history of the shroud as briefly as I could and then showed him the color photographs. He said he knew something about the relic—it seems someone had once approached him about the possibility of carbon-dating it. He said he was interested in doing so, but nothing as yet had come of it.

When I asked him who had approached him, he said he had promised not to reveal the name. Fair enough.

On the basis of what he knew so far, Libby said he favored a chemical explanation for the origin of the images. It was just a hunch, but he didn't think the images had been produced by radiation, unless the radiation were heat waves; but he didn't see how the body, even when alive, could have produced enough heat to cause an image. That would mean postulation of some kind of extra-natural heat—and such a phenomenon would take the whole affair out of the realm of science.

When I mentioned Kirlian photography, Libby replied that one has to be careful in the field of bio-radiation; it's a new field, he explained, and there's much in it that is still speculation.

Before I left, Libby suggested I go down to the basement of his building and observe the equipment with which the Carbon 14 test is administered.

MORE ON KIRLIAN PHOTOGRAPHY

Ralph Graeber had introduced me to Kendall Johnson, a helpful 45-year-old scientific investigator. He was writing a book about Kirlian photography, he told me, after becoming interested in the subject while taking a 1971 course at UCLA, taught by Dr. Thelma Moss. An American psychologist and parasychologist, Moss was intensely interested in human auras and had made trips to Russia to study them.

Johnson, inspired by her class, had subsequently devised a machine to take Kirlian photographs. He showed it to Moss. A partnership developed, experiments were conducted, and the results, once recorded, made them leaders in the field.

Johnson and I were sitting in a UCLA cafeteria examining the shroud photographs; we had just come from the Kirlian Lab set up in the Neuropsychiatric Institute where Dr. Moss had her office.

"There definitely is a similarity here," Johnson said. "The areas of the body that were closest to the shroud show up the darkest, and the areas farther away are lighter."

"This is the negative effect I was telling you about," I said.

"Yes," said Johnson, "even to the point of not showing up at all on the parts that were especially far away."

"You mean the really deep recesses?"

"Yes."

Johnson also noticed something that, so far as I knew, no other shroud researcher had ever reported seeing: faintly visible lines traveling down the entire shroud length. They were clearest down the frontal image and in the center of the images, as in an axis that included the nose, the depression between the two pectoral muscles, the hand with the bloodiest wrist, and the groove between the thighs and the calves. The more we looked, the more lines we found; the entire length of cloth was striated with them.

"We have this, too, in our photos," said Johnson. "It seems to have something to do with the structure of a nearby object like, perhaps, the table upon which the object being photographed is placed. But we're not sure."

Johnson may have seen similarities in the shroud photos and the Kirlian photos, but he didn't say they had both been made by the same thing. In fact, he stressed that he didn't even know exactly how the Kirlian photos were made. "All we know is that we are getting a picture of an unseen structure. This structure is photographed when electrons sense each other's presence and interact."

The interaction could be captured in the sensitive surface of a film or, indeed, on some other surface that was not photosensitive.

"It's the same as when you generate a spark of electricity by walking across a rug and then touch a door knob," he said. "With the right conditions—moisture in the tomb and the unique circumstances of the burial, ointments, and such—you might have had an electrical field generated between the slab he was lying on and the air above the body. Then an image might have formed on the cloth. . . . "

Neither Johnson nor I took this speculation seriously, for several reasons. For example, how would the electricity have been generated in a tomb with no appropriate electrical sources? Johnson thought it extremely doubtful that the shroud images had been formed in exactly the same manner as that in which Kirlian photographs are made. Perhaps, as Graeber believed, the same radiating "energy" had been at work in both phenomena, but Johnson refused to speculate on that.

My next stop was San Francisco. Johnson volunteered to drive me to the airport. On the way he told me about the book he was writing on Kirlian photography, and about how he was supporting himself at the moment by working as an insurance adjustor.

As it so happened, Kirlian photography was the subject of the cover story of the January/February 1974 issue of *The Sciences*, the journal of the New York Academy of Sciences. It focused on the very real possibility that Kirlian photography would be as important a tool in preventive and diagnostic medicine as the discovery of the X-rays and the invention of the electroencephalogram.

LAWRENCE LIVERMORE LABORATORY
• •

After I got off the plane in San Francisco, I rented a car and headed through the green and purple hills of northwestern Alameda County to the flatter country around Livermore, where the Lawrence Livermore Laboratory was located. An abandoned World War II naval air station, the small complex had been taken over in 1950 by the U.S. Atomic Energy Commission to make a laboratory for the production of fissionable material for the development of the first hydrogen bombs. Since that time it had grown to a huge 640-acre, 5,400-employee operation that developed the Polaris, Poseidon, and Minuteman missiles. Beginning in the 1960s, it branched out into peacetime nuclear projects, such as research in nuclear medicine and environmental studies.

Wade Patterson and David S. Myers met me at the reception center, and we walked to a small conference room in the building. Patterson and Myers explained that there was a lot of potentially dangerous radiation at Lawrence, and that their job was to make sure no one got hurt. To do this, they devised and instituted safety measures and monitored levels of radiation absorbed by scientists and their staffs.

Neither of the physicists had ever heard of the shroud before my telephone call a few weeks ago. I gave them a brief rundown on the story and showed them the photographs.

No, they said, they didn't see any way that the shroud images could have been produced naturally by ionizing or high-energy radiation, nuclear or otherwise. X-rays and gamma rays are among the principal ionizing rays, and the images couldn't have been produced by either, because it takes high-voltage machines to generate X-rays, and the only natural sources of gamma rays are radioactive substances like uranium; besides, X-rays and gamma rays don't act on matter in the ways shown on the shroud.

X-rays and gamma rays, they continued, are among the most penetrating radiations; they would have gone right through the shroud instead of marking it. A very intense source of ionizing radiation, they admitted, would have been able to affect the cloth but, given the factors involved—a body, the passage of centuries, and so on—they didn't see how that could have been possible.

Even if, by some unlikely chance, the body had been made radioactive and was therefore emanating X-rays or gamma rays, the images on the shroud were still not in accordance with the kinds of images that should have formed under these circumstances. X-rays and gamma rays are more strongly absorbed by the bones, said Patterson, and thus bones, and not skin, would have been the most distinguishable aspects of the images.

Even if a radioactive substance such as uranium—which emits gamma rays and alpha and beta particles, all of which are ionizing radiations—had been smeared on the body, the scientists still didn't think the shroud images would have appeared; at best, there would have been a silhouette.

If a radioactive substance had been applied in such a way as to emphasize only highlights, they added, they still didn't know of any technique for sensitizing cloth so that it would be able to register high-energy radiation. X-rays were an example of what they meant; film is needed to record the presence of X-rays.

If an atomic blast had gone off over Jerusalem at the time of the burial, there would have been enough high-energy radiation to etch the images on the shroud, but—like the Hiroshima blast—it would have destroyed the shroud itself with its intensity. Even if it didn't destroy the shroud, it would have affected the linen of the shroud in a quite different way.

So much for high-energy, ionizing radiation. But what about low-energy, non-ionizing radiations, I asked the two scientists—such as visible light, infrared, and ultraviolet radiations?

It was conceivable, they were forced to admit, that intense sources of low-energy radiation could have produced the shroud marks by the sheer disposition of heat. But this would be an entirely unnatural situation, since the human body is not known to generate such heat, and since their expertise was not in this area, they did not wish to speculate further on it.

As a parting comment, they suggested that I see a photographic expert at Eastman Kodak in Rochester, New York.

■ ■ ■ ■ ■ ■ ■

Having a little time to kill before my flight from San Francisco to Denver, where I planned to meet with Dr. John Rush, an optical physicist, I tried to find the American representative of the Assyrian Church, supposedly the oldest Christian church in the world. The young priest who answered the door said that the prelate had moved and left no forwarding address. He also said that he knew little about the Church's ancient history.

MEETING WITH DR. RUSH

When I landed at the Denver airport, I rented a car and drove to Boulder, thirty miles away. It was winter, and the snow-covered peaks of the Rockies could be seen the entire way.

I sat down in the living room of a small ranch house in front of a picture window facing the Rockies and showed the shroud photographs to Dr. Rush. He worked with the National Center for Atmospheric Research at the University of Colorado and was a consultant for the Psychical Research Foundation which investigated strange phenomena.

After studying the pictures for a while, Rush said, "You need the cloth, and tests. The thing that gets me, however, is the negative image. It's so good. It has remarkable fidelity."

I explained to him the vapography theory—Vignon's chemical explanation of how the images had formed—and Rush said he was inclined to believe that the images had somehow been formed by chemicals. But he couldn't accept the idea of vapors traveling in straight lines to shape the subtleties of the image, and he was not impressed with the idea that the marks had been scorched into the linen. Ultimately, he admitted he couldn't make any definite remarks about the shroud.

When I told him that the Turin authorities had recently conducted secret tests on the shroud, he looked skeptical. "That's like
the tobacco companies investigating smoking," he said. "They
have too much of a vested interest to be credible." Modern secular science, he added, could do a great deal toward determining
the authenticity of the cloth. He suggested that I see a photo
expert in Tuscon, Arizona.

CHAPTER 15

■■■■■■■■

BACK EAST

FINGERPRINTING THE SHROUD

· ·

Boston *was buried in snow* when my plane arrived. For-
tunately, I had arranged to be met by Richard Orareo, a
35-year-old high school psychologist. I had come across
Orareo's name when I was first doing the newspaper series about
the shroud in 1971, and we had kept in touch ever since. Not
only did he have an excellent knowledge of the shroud story, but
he also owned one of the largest shroud libraries in America, second only, it seemed, to the Wuenschel Collection at Esopus, New
York.

Orareo had bought the library from the estate of Herman
J. Doepner, a fingerprint expert with whom he had been in

correspondence for several years. Doepner had died in August 1971 without realizing his life's dream: publication of a manuscript based on years of research in "identology," a field which he believed provided incontrovertible proof of the authenticity of the shroud.

I hadn't realized the extent of Doepner's involvement with the shroud until I received a letter from his sister, a nun in a St. Paul, Minnesota, convent.

She told me that, during his life, Doepner would organize his entire day around the shroud. Every morning he arose, said a list of prayers devoted to the shroud, and then spent the rest of the day poring over life-size blowups of the shroud figures which he had mail-ordered from London. "He even had an oil painting of Christ hanging in his bedroom," his sister wrote, "which he loved so much that he told my niece he placed it on the wall which received the morning light so that his first glance upon rising would fall upon the picture."

Shroud of Turin Prayer

"Lord Jesus Christ, by the love you bear us, cause the light of your Holy Face to shine upon us always.

Lord, show us your Holy Face and we shall be saved."

Doepner never married, and he lived alone in a country cabin somewhere on the outskirts of St. Paul. For a good part of his young-adult and middle-age years he had researched titles for two St. Paul insurance and real estate firms. In 1926, he became interested in fingerprinting, took it up as a hobby, and by the time of his death had assembled a 1,200-volume fingerprint library which he donated to the International Association of Identification.

Doepner first heard of the shroud in 1952, and in 1956 he retired to devote full time to its study.

His sister wrote:

Seeing "identology" as a discipline uniquely suited to study the various marks on the shroud, he decided to undertake a scientific study of it.... He would prove its authenticity.... To do this, he spent eighteen years studying the markings... purchased every book and photograph of the shroud available... gathered magazine and newspaper articles... allowed no one and nothing to interfere.... He spared no time, effort, or money.

Orareo showed me entire books that Doepner had painstakingly copied, typing page after page, because he could not get anything but a library loan copy for himself, and because he needed them for his study of the shroud.

Precisely what, if anything, Doepner had come up with I couldn't say. I read his manuscript once, hastily, and found one very intriguing hypothesis. He said that, contrary to all previous conceptions, Jesus' body had been laid face down in the tomb, not face up. This theory would explain why the frontal image, and especially the face, was the better etched of the two types of images on the cloth—frontal and dorsal. Somehow pressure, as it is understood in fingerprinting, had been involved—or so he thought.

Orareo was as helpful as he could be. He spent an entire evening digging through his hall closet, bringing out books and articles I thought I might need for my research. When I was ready to leave, I had fifty pounds of written material crammed into various parts of my luggage, all of it Doepner's. And all of it, I felt sure, would prove valuable when I finally sat down to write my book on the shroud.

BROOKLINE

. . . .

The next day I had an appointment with Dr. Constantine Cavarnos, a lecturer on Byzantine icons at the Greek Orthodox

Theological School in Brookline, Massachusetts. Archbishop Iakovos, head of the Greek Orthodox Church in North and South America, had recommended Cavarnos, a layman, as an expert on Eastern Orthodox history.

Cavernos told me about the Edessan legends—the same ones that Wilson and Green were working on in England—but said he was sorry, he didn't see how they were related to the shroud. So far as he knew, the Edessan Image had only a face on it, not an entire body like the shroud. Not unexpectedly, Cavernos didn't know of Wilson's theory that the shroud had been folded like a blanket, with only the head showing.

ANCIENT JEWISH BURIAL CUSTOM

What does the Bible say about the shroud?

What light does ancient Jewish burial custom shed on the story?

These were questions that needed answers.

Edward Wuenschel was one of the few sindonologists who had taken the trouble to consult Jewish experts for information on ancient Jewish burial procedures. The results appeared in his book *Self-Portrait of Christ.*

"To determine what was actually done at the burial of Christ, one must read the whole story as related by the four Evangelists." Matthew, Mark, and Luke gave no indication that the body was washed and wrapped as a mummy; John said that the body was wound in linen cloths in the manner of the Jews, which some Scripture scholars interpret as full ritual washing and mummy wrap. But John's description of what happened can be construed in just the opposite way. Wuenschel writes:

It is reasonable to assume... that the jaw was kept in place by a cloth tied under the chin and over the top of the head—an immemorial practice among all peoples. Many commentators believe that this is what John—in chapter 20, verse 7—means when he refers to "the napkin which was upon his head."

It is reasonable to assume also that Joseph, being a wealthy man and wishing to give Christ a decent burial, brought other linens besides the shroud, intending to use these for swathing the body. Not having time to use them for this purpose, he would naturally leave them in the tomb until after the Sabbath, and we may assume that he placed them beside the body, in rolls or bundles. Thus the body would be "enclosed" in linen cloths—surrounded by the unused swathing bands and enveloped in the shroud—while the head was bound with the jaw-support. The language of John can surely mean this, and it fits in with the rest of the story.

> **The Empty Shroud**
>
> Then Simon Peter came, following him, and went into the tomb; he saw the linen cloths lying, and the napkin, which had been on his head, not lying with the linen cloths but rolled up in a place by itself.
>
> —John 20:6–7

DR. DOV ZLOTNIC

●●●●●●●●●●●●●●●●●●●●●●●

Because Jewish burial customs had been skimpily treated by sindonologists over the years, I had arranged to interview Dr. Dov Zlotnic, professor of rabbinic literature at Manhattan's Jewish Theological Seminary in New York, where the Judaism taught is of the conservative variety. Zlotnic greeted me cordially and bade me sit down. The shelves of books lining the walls made his rather small office look even smaller.

I would have preferred to begin simply by asking questions about Jewish burial customs without revealing why I was doing so. However, since I was dealing with a subject that might eventually lead to a discussion of the resurrection, I decided to tell him the shroud story first and to show him the photographs.

Zlotnic listened attentively and then proposed two solutions. First, couldn't it be an ancient painting that had lost all extraneous paint matter but still retained some coloring? No, I said, and I gave him the reasons why.

Then, he continued, couldn't it be the result of sun shining through a stained-glass window for a long time? Before I could answer in the negative, he retracted the suggestion, agreeing that it couldn't be so, for the reasons already given against the painting theory.

With regard to the ancient burial customs, said Zlotnic, he saw nothing in my description of the shroud that disagreed with them. In order to make any sort of official statement, however, he would have to study the question more thoroughly, something which he couldn't plan to do anytime in the foreseeable future. In the meantime, he said he would have some Xeroxes made of pertinent paragraphs in the seminary library. He also recommended several books on the subject—his own, *The Tractate Mourning*, among them.

Zlotnic then took me to lunch in the seminary cafeteria, where we continued to talk about religions in general. When I asked him if he had ever come across shrouds or burial garments with corpse imprints on them, he answered straightaway, "I know of no burial cloths that have on them any imprint produced by the body. Shrouds will waste away in the course of time, so there can be no hard evidence from antiquity, except where a preservative agent is used."

■■■■■■■■

The only significant piece of hard evidence concerning Jewish burial practices came into my hands after my interview with Zlotnic.

In the March 18, 1960, issue of the *Catholic Herald*, the British sindonologist Vera Barclay pointed out that at the site of the Qumran Community which flourished from the second century BC to 70 AD (and where the Dead Sea Scrolls were found), graves had been uncovered to reveal skeletons in the exact position of the man in the shroud: stretched out flat, face up, and with elbows protruding because of the way the hands had been folded over the pelvic region.

Barclay wrote:

> The significance of the skeletons discovered at Khirbet Qumran in 1951 is that we now have definite confirmation that at the time of Christ, some Jews did bury their dead in the actual position of the shroud images. Note... that the elbows projecting [out] would not have been convenient for the close winding of the Egyptian way.

Jewish Burial Wrappings

How was the linen shroud placed around Jesus' body in the tomb? The four gospels use different Greek verbs that carry varying connotations.

Mark: *eneilesen* (wrapped)

Matthew and Luke: *enetylixen* (wrapped or folded)

John: *edesan* (bound)

Nearly all scholars agree, however, that the gospels show Jesus' body was wrapped loosely in linen, as indicated by the image on the shroud.

CRUCIFIXION: THE CRUELEST DEATH

Having satisfied some of my curiosity regarding Jewish burial customs and, nevertheless, having run out of available experts in that field, I turned my attention to methods of crucifixion. James Carpenter, professor at General Theological Seminary in Manhattan, confirmed my understanding that very little was known about crucifixion.

"Reading the encyclopedias, you'll get about as much knowledge as we have," he told me.

I had gotten Carpenter's name from the *Encyclopedia Americana*, in which he'd written the article on crucifixion. I'd found more information on this hideous form of punishment in various other writings.

For instance, in his book *The History of Torture*, Daniel P. Mannix wrote:

> The Romans invented an almost endless variation in the techniques of crucifixion. Sometimes the victim was nailed by one arm and one leg on an L-shaped pole; sometimes he was crucified head downward—like tradition says St. Peter was. Nero soaked Christians with tar before having them crucified and used them as human torches around his garden at night.

The Romans reserved crucifixion for outcasts: for runaway slaves such as Spartacus, and for political insurgents, as Jesus appeared to be to some. There were three types of crosses: one shaped like a T, one like an X, and another like a dagger with a hilt. As in the case of Jesus, crucifixion was usually preceded by flogging.

Sometimes the victims were nailed to the cross, sometimes they were tied; sometimes they had a footrest, sometimes a small seat.

Bulldozing a hill overlooking Jerusalem in 1968, Israeli construction crews uncovered the tombs of about thirty-five people who had lived around the time of Jesus. One of them, a young man about twenty-five, had been crucified; a seven-inch nail was still stuck through his heel and into a piece of wood. His other bones showed that the nails for the arms had probably been placed between the radius and ulna bones, the two bones that make up the forearm.

Monsignor Giulio Ricci, when I interviewed him in Turin, gave me his own theory about the crucifixion of Jesus, which he had developed from his lifelong study of the marks on the shroud.

"His hands were tied to the crossbeam, shoulder-high, and thus he couldn't have protected himself when he stumbled," Ricci told me. "Whenever he fell, he would have landed on his face. Judging from some of the contusions on it, it appears he tried to turn his face to avoid the bruises, but he wasn't able to do it very well. The beam must have been in the way. I think eventually he would have died from concussion if the soldiers hadn't stopped it and made Simon of Cyrene carry the cross. They didn't do this out of compassion for Jesus, but because they didn't want him to die on the way to Golgotha. His death was a political matter. It was important that he die as an outlaw. And so the soldiers charged with carrying out the crucifixion didn't want to be held responsible if he didn't die that way."

How long would death by crucifixion have taken?

According to Dr. Hermann Moedder, a German radiologist who got university students to volunteer for a test in which they were tied to a cross, the victim would lose consciousness in no more than twelve minutes. An American sindonologist, Reverend Peter Weyland, S.V.D., has lasted longer lashed to a cross. He told his story in *A Sculptor Interprets the Holy Shroud of Turin*, published in 1954.

Weyland writes:

> I set up a large cross and placed a large refinished mirror on the wall in front of it. Thus equipped, I experimented with hanging on the cross from 700 to 800 times for short intervals to observe how a body, fastened with hands and feet and without the use of a footrest or a seat, would hang.

Weyland had first read of the shroud in a 1934 book, *The Holy Shroud of Turin*, by Monsignor Arthur S. Barnes, an Oxford University chaplain and a former editor of the *Dublin Review*, published in Ireland. In the book, Barnes maintained that Jesus' body was wrapped in the shroud on Golgotha, and that the images had been transferred to the shroud cloth as the body was carried to the tomb. After reading the book, Weyland began giving lantern slide lectures about the shroud and learning the mechanics of hanging. In 1937, Father Wuenschel asked him to model a crucifix, using the shroud data as a basis for his measurements. He accepted willingly and plunged into the task.

"I decided to make plaster casts of portions of the body while hanging. Thirty-one suspensions, lasting from twenty to twenty-five minutes each, were needed to round out two complete sets of casts covering the whole body."

These casts, and the photographs Weyland took during the shorter suspensions, served as models for the crucifixes he fashioned.

THERMOGRAPHY

My research on crucifixion gave me a clearer idea of how Jesus had died. It was a terrible ordeal, one of the worst ever recorded, glossed over in the mind sometimes because of its almost matter-of-fact presentation in the New Testament. The shroud images, however, were still the main question. How had they been made? Heat, even scorch, had been suggested, although not the kind that would actually burn, but more like a subtle, light-derived ray. X-rays, then, still seemed worth looking into, and New York had some of the best radiologists in the world.

When I approached Dr. Edith Quimby, a radiologist at New York's Columbia University Medical School, she willingly agreed to give me whatever help she could, as had Professor Carpenter when I'd left him. Dr. Quimby had been recommended to me by the Miami radiologist, Harold Davis.

After hearing the shroud story and examining the photographs, she said she didn't have the slightest idea how the images could have been formed.

When I broached the possibility that the images looked as though they might have been produced by scorching, she suggested I see Dr. Ernest Wood, a radiologist at the Neurological Institute of New York; he was an expert in thermography, the use of bodily heat in diagnostic medicine. Dr. Quimby called him and made an appointment for me.

■ ■ ■ ■ ■ ■ ■ ■

Thermography, explained Dr. Ernest Wood, grew out of infrared photography, which was developed in World War II; today it is used mainly in the detection of breast cancer. The principle behind it is a simple one: heat emanating from the body is used to make diagnostic pictures, and the pictures are negatives.

But there were significant differences, Dr. Wood pointed out, between thermographic pictures and the "pictures" on the shroud. For one thing, it took sophisticated machines to magnify body heat to the extent that a picture could be registered—the magnification was on the order of one million times. For another, the thermographic picture was registered on Polaroid film, not cloth.

The negative was not exactly the same either. The reason the film showed a negative image was that the prominences of the body—nose, cheeks, forehead—were closer to the camera and consequently reflected more heat than recesses like the eye socket. Since heat is what showed up on the film, the prominences would be dark, as in a photographic negative. If, however, something were wrong in one of the recesses—for example, if there were an eye infection—that recess would give off more heat and show darker on the film than even the prominences; thus the resulting pictures would not be true negatives.

THE LAST TO KNOW

Filmmaker George Suski was next on my list. I couldn't blame him for being angry. He had invested hundreds of thousands of dollars making a color film about the shroud story, and he didn't even have a color shot of the relic in it; apparently no one told him about the 1973 exposition. I told him when I came to New York I'd stop by.

Talking with him at the offices of Suski Productions, I learned that he had taken a film crew to England and Italy and had interviewed several sindonologists, the most prominent of whom was Giovanni Judica-Cordiglia. But Cordiglia, I had come to realize, was regarded as "old school" by modern sindonologists, part of the rigid shroud-governing group in Turin. Many newer sindonologists blamed this group for the lack of modern testing of the shroud. But that was infighting, and I was an outsider, so I tried not to take sides. Regarding the film, the interviews were fine, but with or without color shots of the cloth, it didn't appear to me to reflect the tremendous depth of the shroud story. It was, in my opinion, the sort of film one might see as a student in a high school auditorium.

"By the way," Suski said as I was leaving his office, "you don't know when the next exposition will be, do you?"

Also angry was Thomas Humber, a freelance writer and editor who was preparing a manuscript on the shroud. Months before the television exposition of the shroud in November 1973, he requested permission to be present, along with other members of the press, with the scholars, clergy, and scientists.

"I volunteered to obey any strictures that might be placed on my presence. I wanted, indeed I needed, to see the mysterious ancient cloth that had for so long occupied my thoughts. In spite of the efforts of Father Rinaldi, who made every effort on my behalf, I was told that no outsiders would be allowed to access the shroud, that there would be no press conference, and that no one would be admitted to the cathedral when the cloth was displayed other than the television crew and Turin officials."

In *The Fifth Gospel: The Miracle of the Holy Shroud*, which was published by Pocket Books in 1974, Humber went on to say, "I was thus faced with an expensive and frustrating journey, only to sit in a hotel room and see the shroud on Italian television. I decided not to go."

I'd been faced with the same decision. Encouraged by Father Rinaldi, I'd luckily decided to go.

LEN BARCUS

• • • • • • • • • • • • • • • • •

The last expert on my New York list was Len Barcus, an astronomer, inventor, and optical physicist. He had been recommended to me by Dr. Karlis Osis, head of the American Society of Psychical Research, for whom he had developed some testing gadgetry.

Barcus met me at the train station in New Rochelle, and during the short drive from the station to his house, he filled me in on his background. With degrees in mathematics and astronomy from the University of Virginia, he taught at Columbia University. After World War II, he developed optical instrumentation for viewing stars in daylight from high-flying aircraft.

Sitting at the dining-room table in his home, I told the shroud story for what seemed the thousandth time and showed him the shroud photographs. Simple contact, that's how the images were made, he said: simple contact with a corpse. When I told him how contact experiments by Vignon and Judica-Cordiglia had failed to reproduce sharp images, Barcus persisted. He dropped a handkerchief over a bust on a pedestal; then he realized that although the basic features would come out, the subtleties, the curves, the depression which would give the image a lifelike quality, would not.

"Yes, it is puzzling, isn't it?" he said, backing away from the bust.

The scorch theory interested him next. I was about to present the first objection to the scorch theory—namely, that the cloth wasn't damaged—when he said that a single burn was simple oxidation. When a hot iron momentarily touches a sheet, the singe, or scorch, that results causes oxidation or browning to occur. The same thing happens, he went on to explain, when shrimp are dropped into boiling water; the only visible change is that the shrimp turn a darker shade of pink.

Perhaps, I mused later, the images on the shroud had not been scorched onto the linen; maybe they were cooked on. But I wasn't a scientist, and I was running out of experts.

CHAPTER 16

■■■■■■■■

DRAWING CONCLUSIONS

*B*ack in Miami, having interviewed* as many sindonologists and shroud enthusiasts as I could find, and having
consulted as many experts in the sciences touching upon
the shroud, I could now contemplate the two major problems—
the authenticity of the shroud and the origin of the images on the
shroud—and draw conclusions I never could have dreamed of
twelve months ago.

First, the cloth is unique. Nowhere in my wanderings did I
come across a burial cloth, or the record of a burial cloth, with
body imprints.

Second, the imprinted cloth is old, at least 600 years old as the
"shroud of Turin," probably nearly 2,000 years old as the
"Image of Edessa."

Third, the linen of the cloth and the herringbone twill could have been manufactured and distributed throughout the Mediterranean world at least 2,000 years ago.

Fourth, the imprints on the cloth are those of a real corpse in rigor mortis. This is the testimony of numerous pathologists. So precise is the anatomical realism, said Vignon, that separation of serum and cellular mass—a true characteristic of dried blood—is evident in many of the blood stains. Swelling, the natural reaction of a live body to injury, is seen in the bruises on the face. Rigor mortis is evident in the enlarged chest (from his strivings for air) and distended feet. The feet were flush with the upright, and remained in that abnormal position when the body was taken down.

Fifth, the man in the shroud was mutilated in exactly the same manner that the New Testament says Jesus was. He was crucified, scourged with a Roman flagrum, lacerated around the head as if with thorns, and beaten about the face. He also has an excoriated shoulder, such as a crossbeam might make. All of these wounds, say pathologists, were inflicted when the man was alive. They show swelling. But the stab wound in the chest—which corresponds to what a Roman lance might make—came, as the New Testament says Jesus' did, after death. There is no swelling around it.

Sixth, the man was interred in the manner of the Jews—that is, in a linen shroud—but he did not receive the ritual washing, as the New Testament indicates Jesus did not.

Seventh, the odds against someone other than Jesus—one of the many others crucified in ancient times—coincidentally being whipped, beaten, crowned with thorns, stabbed in the side, and interred in the exact manner Jesus was (and that this ancient unknown's shroud would have been preserved) are 225 billion to 1, according to Paul de Gail, a French Jesuit priest and engineer. Italian physicist Tino Zeuli, who quoted de Gail in the April 1974 issue of *Sindon*, went on to liken the possibility to a brick in the street suddenly sprouting wings and taking off.

But couldn't the shroud images just be the result of a clever fake? Couldn't someone have taken a body and purposefully mutilated it to look like Jesus?

Not likely. The forger would have had to acquire a body more alive than dead, then mutilate it according to the quite specific details in the Gospels—even to the degree of actually hoisting the live body onto a horizontal cross.

Barbet pointed out that the downward direction of the blood flows on the arms and the large, curling stain on the forehead indicate that blood flowed and clotted while the man was in an upright position, with arms outstretched and slightly above his head. The downward flows, as the welling in the wrinkles of the forehead show, even followed the natural body contours.

Even if the forger had taken such unnecessary pains and had known such relatively obscure and unobvious details, he then would have had to have known how to do something that has never been done before, even to this day: namely, transfer the image of the dead man onto the cloth in such a way that it resembled a perfect photographic negative—and this without photography (the positive with which to check his work) to guide him.

But how would he do this? By pressing a cloth to the front and back of the body? Vignon and Judica-Cordiglia were unable to do it this way, even in a relatively modern laboratory. Could he then use the corpse as a model and paint the image onto the cloth? No pigment has ever been detected on the threads—not even the hint of a brush stroke. And art experts who have looked at it swear it's not an artistic creation. Artists, they say, couldn't do it.

But assuming that the forger somehow did know how to make such a unique image, why would he have done so? We know the cloth is at least 600 years old, so no one, including the artist himself, would have been able to appreciate his work (the startling positive image) until photography was invented—at least 500 years later.

In addition, the forger working in France (or thereabouts) around 1350 most probably would have to have been either an overzealous monk whose piety got the better of him, or an arrogant swindler who wanted to make a bundle in the underground relic market. But both of these possibilities seem unlikely, since the portrayal of Jesus on the shroud is nontraditional and non-European.

The man in the shroud was crowned with a "cap" of thorns, rather than the traditional "wreathlet." He was nailed in the wrists, not in the palms. And he is naked. Seldom in traditional Christian art does one see depictions of Jesus without a loincloth.

And yet these same details are highly realistic when considering that the real Jesus would have been mutilated and crucified in the Eastern manner, and by professional crucifiers. In the East, the traditional crown is a miter, which resembles a cap. Barbet proved that nails in the palms would not support the weight of a hanging body. But when the nails were put in the wrists between the collection of bones around what he called "Destot's Space," the body held fast as if in a vice. Finally, crucifixion was meant to be a degrading death. Not only would professional crucifiers have put the nails in the wrists, but experts on the torture agree they would have stripped their victims naked. But a thirteenth-century forger would probably have been burned at the stake for depicting Jesus thus.

Eighth, the random victim and forger's work thus considered, it is therefore not unreasonable to conclude that the man in the shroud is indeed the historical person we call Jesus Christ. Such a person did exist, most historians will agree. And since his ministry gave rise to the largest religion in the world, it is not so unusual to think we might have some material evidence of him.

Ninth, that Jesus is the man in the shroud, however, does not in and of itself prove or disprove that Jesus came back to life and rose from the dead. But there are indications that, at the least, something very unusual occurred in the cloth.

The images are unique and inexplicable. And due to the absence of stains of decomposition on the linen, we know that the body exited the shroud prior to putrefaction—exactly what the New Testament says Jesus' body did. But how? It doesn't seem possible that the cloth could have been unwrapped without messing the "picture-perfect" bloodstains. (If they were wet, the slightest jar would have smudged them. If they were dry, then not only they but the cloth itself—since they would have been enmeshed in it— would have been damaged.) And "picture-perfect" suggests light radiation, as in photography and photographic negative.

RETURN TO THE TOMB

To get some appreciation of what is held as theological fact by many, one must reconstruct what happened during those thirty-six hours or so after Jesus' death.

The tomb, a rocky chamber carved out of a hillside, a stone rolled against the door, is dark and silent. Lying on a slab is a long, rectangular cocoon, the hills and valleys of which are clearly the contours of a human body. The body of Jesus lies there, face up, a ribbon around the head and chin to keep the mouth closed, packed on all sides with bags of spices.

At some unknown moment in the dead of night, the air in the tomb becomes electric.

At first the vibrations are minute, the sort that could be detected by sensitive twentieth-century instruments; then they dramatically increase until they shake the ground and blow the boulder from the door.

A glow, faint at first, emanating from the shroud suddenly intensifies until rays of light shoot through the threads, star-filled golden rays filling the tomb and pouring out the door.

For thirty seconds—no more—the blinding, pulsating movement continues.

The source of the activity is the corpse, the body, somehow being revitalized, dematerialized, its mass being converted into energy, pure energy, which in the material world is radiant white light.

The body rises from the slab through the cloth, hovers for a moment in midair, then disappears.

The cocoon collapses. Darkness returns. Shouts of "Earthquake! Earthquake!" diminish as the guards run for their lives. And in the air, the distinct odor of scorched linen.

When dawn comes, the women in Jesus' life draw tentatively toward the tomb, look in the opening, and see the shroud unopened, still wrapped, but definitely deflated. The body is gone. At sunrise the disciples come. John enters the tomb, puts his hand on the cloth, and presses it to the slab. Jesus is there no longer. The disciples and the women quickly gather up the burial garments— the chin band is still inside the shroud—and the spice bags and leave before the Romans can return.

At another time, in another place, when they have a chance to gather their wits, they will discover the figure of their master imprinted on the inside of the shroud. The images would be faint, probably not as dark as the passage of time and exposure to air have made them; and the images would be negative ones, a phenomenon that would also become clearer with the passage of time.

Regardless, they would view these images as holy—imprints of their precious Lord. The disciples would pay more attention to the images on the shroud if they weren't already waiting, with the greatest anticipation, for Jesus himself, who, before his death, had promised to visit them after he rose from the dead.

PART III
2010

■■■■■■■■

THE MYSTERY
CONTINUES

CHAPTER 17

■■■■■■■■

THE SHROUD CONDEMNED

THE 1988 CARBON 14 TEST

●●●●●●●●●●●●●●●●●●●●●●●●●●●●●●●●

*I*n 1988 *Carbon 14 dating tests* were performed on a small, non-image portion of the shroud. The results were negative for the Christ Era. The three labs doing the tests—the University of Arizona, Britain's Oxford University, and Switzerland's Federal Institute of Technology in Zurich—all concluded that the tiny portion of the sample each had received from the lower left corner of the relic had originated almost without question (95 percent certainty) between 1260 and 1380 AD.

The news was a blow to those who thought the cloth much older, especially those scientifically attracted. Science is modern-day king, and despite the shroud's many unsolved mysteries, the news stung. The Vatican, and especially the Turin archdiocese, seemed to accept the verdict. Rubbing it in, archeologist and art expert, the late Oxford Professor Edward Hall, a declared agnostic and advisor to the tests, dismissed the shroud on British television "as a load of rubbish," likening believers to "flat-earthers."

It was a stinging rebuke, picked up with other slights by the world's press, which in general was trumpeting the news that the shroud was a medieval fake. No argument. No other side presented. Radio Carbon dating, to journalists, trumped all other evidence. *Time* magazine mockingly titled its October 24, 1988, article, "Debunking the Shroud of Turin." Tests "prove" it's not Jesus' cloth, added the subhead. The *New York Times*'s headline (September 22, 1988) said "Fraud." To be fair, *Time* at least said, "Questions remain." Most other reports simply trashed the linen, many with relish. This was an enlightened age. How could believers be so stupid?

After the initial shock, sindonogists tried to fight back.

Contamination was a distinct possibility, wrote Dr. Eugenia Nitowski, a Holy Land archaeologist and Utah-based Catholic nun (T.O.R.C.H. October–November 1988).

Nitowski wrote:

We know the [shroud] has been touched [even kissed] by thousands of people, exposed to uncounted hours of candle smoke and direct sun, littered with fibers from ... other fabrics .... [It] survived a major fire (1532) ... [was] doused with water ... and contained a human corpse which has coated the cloth with all the substances of death, including blood, myrrh, aloe, and the calcium of the rock-cut tomb.

The 1532 fire alone could have changed the carbon content, noted John Tyler, a textile expert writing in the bulletin of the

British Society for the Turin Shroud (October 1988). The fire was so hot the silver casket containing the shroud had melted. That only happens at 960 degrees Centigrade, Tyler wrote. Moisture in the cloth would have turned to steam. Contaminants would have dissolved "and been forced not only into the weave and yarn, but also into the [individual linen] fibers." They would have "become part of the chemistry of the ... [fibers]. ... impossible to remove by surface actants and ultrasonic cleaning," which presumably the Carbon 14 testers had employed.

The sample itself was suspect, argued William Meacham, a U.S. archeologist at the University of Hong Kong, who had been involved in the test planning. All three samples of the shroud had been taken from a corner that was suspected to have been repaired. Good testing is always done on a variety of samples, he said, and samples also should have been cut from *undamaged* areas as well. In fact, that was the original plan, said Meacham, as well as having seven—not just a meager three—labs performing the tests in varied procedures rather than all in the same manner, as had been done. Why had the original plans been abandoned? In a further piece of intrigue, Meacham, who would later author a book entitled *The Rape of the Turin Shroud*, disclosed to a French wire service reporter, Sinan Fisek, that a shroud thread acquired in 1973 had secretly been dated from between 200 AD and 1000 AD, a conflicting outcome showing the need for further testing.

In 1973, the day after the first ever television showing of the actual shroud (on Italian television), Turin's Cardinal Pellegrino had secretly permitted a small commission of experts to privately examine the linen. Among them was Belgian Professor Gilbert Raes, a textile expert, who was allowed to snip a tiny sample of the cloth from an area adjacent, it would turn out, to the corner area from which the Carbon 14 sample had later been taken. This tiny "Raes" sample, later making its way to several sindonologists, had been dated surreptitiously in 1982 at a California university, as Meacham told Fisek. "The results were never announced," he said, "because the test was conducted without the permission of the Turin church authorities."

Of course there was need to verify such an unofficial test, about which there was controversy. (The university in question denied the tests had been made at all, while the tester admitted to sindonologists that he had done it.) The issue is still in debate. But even without it, there were further reasons for caution about the 1988 tests.

THE SHROUD OF TURIN RESEARCH PROJECT

For instance, in 1978, a group of approximately thirty-five scientists from prestigious organizations, including agnostics, Jews, and skeptics, had been so intrigued by the shroud's properties, that they had formed a study group called The Shroud of Turin Research Project, or STURP. Because of their credibility and potential in possibly providing answers, they, for the first time amongst petitioners to the Turin authorities, had been given permission to perform tests on the linen, albeit only nondestructive tests. For five intensive days in Turin they probed the cloth, using high-powered, special microscopes, ultraviolet light, low power X-rays, fluorescence photography, and chemical analysis, including of meager samples of blood and tape-gathered debris they were allowed to take from the shroud's surface. In a 1981 press conference at New London, Connecticut, they declared that the blood on the shroud tested "positively" for blood components hemoglobin and serum albumin, meaning the blood was real. They also declared that their peer-reviewed analysis showed the image was that of an authentic "scourged and crucified man . . . not the product of an artist."

The scientists had found no paint, dye, stain, or other outside coloring matter in the images. The images consisted solely of "degraded cellulose" or "oxidized" (aged and hardened), "dehydrated" (demoisturized), and "conjugated" (molecularly changed) linen fibers. The degrading, characterized as a yellow-brown "carmelization," had occurred only on the outside upper areas of each fiber—in effect, on the tips. It had not penetrated the fibers and was not on the lower stems. This negated the use of paint or dye or other liquids, because such coloring agents would have been absorbed into the interior of each tiny fiber through capillary action, and/or would have flowed down its minute length.

Variations in shading in the image—for instance, the fact that the prominence of the nose is darker than its sides, or the recesses of the eyes are lighter than the nose bridge—is determined only by the clumping together of the image fibers, not by a difference in the amount of

> ## How Could an Artist Do This?
>
> Scientists agree that the images on the shroud of Turin could not have been painted on. Interestingly, the images are only on the surface of the linen. Daniel R. Porter writes on his website shroudstory.com, "[T]he implementation of the coloring is more like lines used for shading in an engraving. The lines are on the surface only, on fibers that are a fraction of the width of a single hair in a fine artist's paint brush." Thick paint would have coated the outer fibers of the shroud, while thin paint or dye would have seeped through to the other side. Porter goes on to say, "You can see the thin coat of color through a microscope and it is hard to imagine how an artist could have accomplished this."

carmelization or degrading covering each fiber tip. There absolutely was no brush stroke. The degrading of each fiber was uniform throughout. The image was formed by more or less degraded fibers together. The more the fibers were clumped together, the darker the image appeared; less clumping resulted in a lighter image.

In addition, the scientists had confirmed a startling new earlier finding that the image had three-dimensional (3-D) information encoded on it. The clumping of degraded fibers was so uniform and precise that a computer could translate the lighter and darker groupings into mathematically precise values, which enabled STURP members Dr. John Jackson, a physicist, and Dr. Eric Jumper, an engineer, both officers and scientists at the U.S. Air Force Weapons Laboratory, Albuquerque, New Mexico, to make a three-dimensional model of the man in the shroud. They did this by feeding the encoded values of the various groupings into a VP-8 image analyzer, a device normally used by the National Aeronautics and Space Administration (NASA) to make raised relief maps from non-traditional, electronic photos of distant planets. (Because the distances were so far, such photos were not taken by conventional cameras using traditional light-sensitive film, but by cameras tabulating emitted light photons.)

With the encoded information, a computer could plot exactly how the shroud lay over the figure; where it touched and didn't touch. The computer did this by revealing minute but precise distances between the man and the cloth. Where the shroud touched his body, the degraded fibers were clumped the most; less so where there was space between the cloth and body. The lightest parts of the image had the least number of clumped fibers. In this way, the computer plotted the peaks and valleys on the head, torso, arms, and other aspects of the frontal, dorsal, and side images.

"Astonishingly," Jackson's website says (in an article entitled "The Shroud and Modern Science"), "the relief [3-D] image [on the analyzer's screen] looked quite anatomically plausible, even down to the subtle details of the face." No known paintings or traditional photographs have ever yet yielded such encoded values and do not produce three-dimensional images. "Eyes protrude, noses sink, and other distortions graphically testify to the uniqueness of the Shroud image," wrote STURP members Kenneth E. Stevenson and Gary R. Habermas in their 1981 book, *Verdict on the Shroud*.

The three-dimensionality forced the idea of an artist's steady hand—even his or her creativity—into the realm of absurdity. It meant the artist would have had to create the image with methods unknown and undetectable even to twentieth-century science, in an absurd, unrecognized (until photography) negative style, and with microscopic uniformity and precision, on millions of tiny cloth fibers many times thinner than human hairs. What artist could do that? "Controlled experiments with highly trained artists have demonstrated that the human eye-brain-coordination system is incapable of both recognizing and creating an intensity correlation (the mathematically precise lighter and darker values) to the degree found on the Shroud," says Jackson's website.

The 3-D encoding also appeared to negate the image being like a conventional photograph. Traditional cameras record reflections of light (more light causing brightness, less causing shadows) to make an image. But the shroud images didn't depend on light (unless light had caused the precision degrading of the fibers). Rather, the "picture" on the shroud was made up of uniformly degraded fibers grouped like pixels (tiny dots) in a computer image, the number of pixels together determining lightness or darkness and thereby etching the image. The image just happened to look like a photographic negative. In reality, it was a mathematically precise map of how the body contacted the cloth.

But none of this seemed to register with the mainstream press. To them, the shroud was simply a clever con—a fake somehow created by a medieval forger who could manipulate paint (or an unknown primitive camera with space-age precision) in a way that made no sense to his contemporaries. Forget the large body of evidence in medicine, archeology, history, and art pointing toward an earlier date. Forget the profound mysteries of how the image was made and how the body somehow exited the shroud without disturbing the picture-perfect blood clots.

Forget that the Carbon 14, a relatively new test, might be suspect.

As a kind of coup de grâce, the opposition theory of Walter McCrone, the Chicago debunker of the Vinland Map, was given undue weight. McCrone was not involved in STURP's 1978 testing. But the scientists, eager for informed input, gave him specimens and post-test membership.

To their surprise—because he did not report it first to them as they had asked and expected— McCrone publicly announced he had found iron oxide, a frequent ingredient of ancient paint, on the cloth, and invoked the forgotten d'Arcis documents. Both, he declared, proved the shroud was a thirteenth-century painting. Vexed, STURP members went back to their labs to check for the iron oxide, denouncing McCrone for

> **The Church's Response to McCrone's Findings:**
>
> "You are the one person to challenge the enduring mystery of the Shroud. The Turin Center of Sindonology [a.k.a. Catholic Church] accepts the challenge from you.... We are all in a challenging mood in Turin, having fought and won many a battle."

not publishing his findings in peer-reviewed professional journals as they had.

As it turned out, the scientists agreed there might be traces of iron oxide on the cloth. That would be expected given the shroud's history of being displayed in so many ancient cathedrals and palaces, each draped with art. What they suspected McCrone found, however, were tiny blood particles from the blood already on the shroud which had broken off and been distributed on the linen from the cloth's repeated handling and folding through the centuries. The image certainly wasn't the result of painting, the scientists continued to insist, for the reasons they'd documented. McCrone, however, did not waiver. He continued to assert in popular, non-peer-reviewed articles and documentaries that the image had been painted. He did this until his death in 2002.

Thus, the suspect Carbon 14 tests, the media's ignorance of the cloth's unique mysteries, and McCrone's findings which were given undue weight by a largely uninformed public were main contributors to forcing the shroud back into relative obscurity.

But as had so often happened in the past, the shroud, in due time, was again to be resurrected.

CHAPTER 18

∎∎∎∎∎∎∎∎

DIVINE VOICES, HARD SCIENCE

W*hatever the Shroud's origin*, its existence today, considering all it has been through, is remarkable. Even if its undocumented but probable history is dismissed—surviving early Christian persecutions, a devastating flood in sixth-century Edessa, brutal Moslem conquests, and the 1204 sacking of Constantinople—its *known* history is rife with escapes from angry denouncements and physical disasters. It was condemned by Catholic bishops in fourteenth-century France, rescued from a devastating fire in 1532, and dismissed as a fake and product of later photo lab chicanery at the dawn of the twentieth century, only to be redeemed in 1931 after new photos confirmed the positive-negative nature of its images. During World War II it escaped searching Nazis, and as recently as 1997, it was rescued from certain destruction in an arsonist's fire just prior to being exhibited in Turin.

The Shroud Survives an Arsonist's Fire

Most recently, on April 11, 1997, the shroud escaped another fire. Turin's royal chapel and cathedral, where the shroud is kept, caught fire sometime before 11:45 p.m. that night. (Although not certain at first, it was later determined that the fire had been set by an arsonist.) Rescuers, led by fireman Mario Trematore, broke through the bullet-proof glass case enclosing the shroud, using first a sledgehammer and then their gloved hands, and saved it from the flames.

Such longevity alone speaks to the relic's uniqueness. Few artifacts, sacred or profane, have survived to thrive again even more than before. And, as the twenty-first century dawned, a strange turn of events has once again given new life to the shroud. While sindonologists continued their studies in spite of the damning Carbon 14, none could truthfully say a really powerful challenge to the 1988 death knell had been mounted until a diminutive but determined woman (who had not heard of the shroud until 1997) got involved. Her name was M. Sue Benford, a medical nurse and former world-class athlete who, as controversial as some of her methods were, uncovered, along with her sindonologist partner (a former Benedictine monk), important new evidence that the linen cloth is more ancient than the Carbon 14 tests suggest.

A PAINFUL CHILDHOOD

Benford's story, according to her 2002 book *Strong Woman: Unshrouding the Secrets of the Soul*, really—because of how it propelled her—begins in the hell of childhood cancer. It was 1962. She was five and diagnosed with a malignant kidney tumor. Survival rates then for that cancer, she writes, were less than 10 percent. Her parents, grieving and willing to try anything, entered her into a hospital's experimental treatment of surgery, radiation, and chemotherapy. There were no support groups. A hush-hush attitude was prevalent about what was happening. Parents were not allowed, as they are today, to stay overnight with their children. Chemotherapy, chillingly, was administered after the parents had left, while the children were alone.

Benford remembered "nights watching my parents walk out of the room, then lying awake waiting for the doctors to come in with my shot." Sometimes the awful "poison" would leak from the entered vein causing agonizing flesh burns. Worse, she writes, was the "overpowering nausea and vomiting." Her bed would fill from retching, while her nurse's light sometimes went unanswered until the morning, "just before my mother arrived." Because the staff had told her it would hurt less if she were a "good" girl, and her mother had said she couldn't bear it if her daughter wasn't "strong and brave," the little girl decided never to protest or cry. In effect, she stifled her emotions. "For two years I laid stoically quiet and still throughout."

After surgery and complications, she had shrunk to an emaciated, stomach-scarred thirty-two pounds, "fighting for my life." When her mother attempted suicide following her recovery, Benford wrongly felt it was her fault and vowed from that time on always to do whatever it took to make her loved ones happy. This determination, coupled with the emotional shutdown which continued, factored into two bad marriages, first to an abusive alcoholic and the second to a hidden philanderer whom she finally, to her shock, discovered. In the meantime, she became a nurse helping children in cancer wards and, to build her broken body and spirit, a competing powerlifter who, after suffering the brunt of cruel gym jokes, rose to capture world records, including a 338.4- pound deadlift in the 97-pound women's division.

VISIONS

. . . .

It was while struggling in the gym that Benford first experienced what would eventually lead her to the shroud. She calls it an "insight" which manifested itself as an inner voice. "Arise to the challenge," it said. "I am with you." In effect, she did rise, becoming a champion. But it wasn't until years later, following the breakup of her second marriage and the resultant inner turmoil, that she visited a psychic of Catholic background who, she writes, "amazed" her with knowledge of her private, personal life. She'd gotten this knowledge, the psychic said, from Sue's accompanying "angelic guides." Benford didn't know what to make of this, but to learn more she attended the psychic's workshop on spiritual advancement through meditation and "visitation." Eventually, she writes, she was able, in a meditative state, to communicate with the unseen guides who, at least in her mind, identified themselves as the Apostle John—and Jesus. (She records that John came first, while Jesus was introduced to her later.)

"One night, at the beginning of my meditation," she writes, "I relayed my desire to meet Jesus to John. He nodded his head, gave a big smile, and moved back to one side. Behind him stood the most magnificent being I had ever encountered. His image was bathed in a brilliant white light. I knew it was Jesus Christ, the Son of God. Being in his presence was so powerful and awe inspiring that I literally began to cry and shrank to the level of a small infant."

Reality? Hallucination?

Whatever the truth, she believed it. And the meditative visitations changed her life. John and Jesus, she writes, told her she was on a journey to elevate her soul, as are all humans. The ultimate goal is unrequited love, which is God's love. It may take many lifetimes. Everything that happens, including the bad, such as her childhood cancer, is for the purpose of teaching and elevating. The soul learns and grows this way. There was much more. Unversed in religion, Benford studied the Bible and, she writes, at the suggestion of Jesus, early Christian Gnostics rejected by the Church. They had truths too, he told her.

"A whole new world was opening to me," she wrote, "thrilling, simple, complex, and alarming." Trained as she was "in the hard sciences as a nurse," she wondered, "How could my non-religious brain have conjured all of this?" But "revelations" (one that saved her mother from a deadly brain aneurysm, and another that preserved her own eyesight), among other happenings for which she had no other explanation, convinced her that the visitations were real. Her confidence and knowledge grew, as did her wellbeing. She emerged from the emotional cocoon she'd been in since childhood.

■ ■ ■ ■ ■ ■ ■ ■

One night, exhausted, Benford heard a voice command, "Go watch TV." Not knowing if it was just weariness, she plopped on the couch and began channel surfing. She came upon a shroud documentary. "My heart lurched...It was him!...Jesus...the same person I had been conversing with all these months." That it was the same face was undeniable. She scribbled what she could and called her psychic advisor, who told her not to waste her time. The shroud was a fake. It had been made in the Middle Ages.

During her next meditation, Benford asked Jesus about the cloth. "Not only did he confirm its authenticity...but he said,

'You will tell the world how the image was created and what it means.'"

She rebelled. "It was the most studied artifact in human history," she argued. She wasn't a scientist. She wasn't even a Catholic! But believing she'd been ordered, she offered "a deal." If Jesus would provide proof, she'd do it. She thought that would get her off the hook. But Jesus, she writes, simply responded, "All right."

JOINING WITH A MONK

Until that point, Benford had avoided the Internet. But if she was going to be able to do what Jesus wanted—namely, if she was to pave the way for the shroud to be declared authentic—she needed to know everything about it. Early on in her research, she ran into mentions of Dr. John Jackson, one of the founders of STURP. Earlier, as she had studied the Bible, she had written several articles on subjects other than the shroud, which were published in church publications. For instance, she wrote one about the great flood. These articles were at least a way of showing her research abilities. Would Dr. Jackson work with her? Summoning courage, she called. But Jackson's wife, who answered the phone, Benford writes, told her he was too busy to talk and referred her to an acquaintance, Fr. Joseph Marino, a Catholic priest, sindonologist, and Benedictine monk who had aided them in the past.

A monk? Now she really needed courage.

What Benford didn't know was that Marino, who had one of the best private collections of shroud literature in the United States, felt that studying and lecturing about the shroud, which he'd been doing for some twenty years, was one of the most important activities in his life. Benford and Marino hit it off. "For some odd unexplainable reason," she wrote, "I felt extremely comfortable with this voice on the other end of the phone." She held nothing back and told him about her visitations and insights. "I could tell he was cautious but intrigued." At his end, he later told me in an interview, "I found her very erudite," and after more phone calls and an exchange of emails and reading some of her articles, "we just quickly formed a bond."

And, in fact, after a year of growing email and phone communication (during which time Sue traveled with him to a parish to meet with Marino's spiritual advisor, a diocesan priest, which resulted in the advisor's blessing), Marino would leave the order and eventually marry Sue. It was not a decision easily reached. On her end, Benford kept getting insights that Marino might be a partner in her mission but, because of his vocation, was reluctant to believe it could happen. Meanwhile Marino was having sleepless nights over the possibility of leaving the monastery because of the growing situation. It was a huge step in his life. But Sue's revelations about him, he says, kept coming true. Although continuing to be separated for a year as he grappled with the problem, they grew closer. Spiritually, they were of the same mind.

Marino told me, "She said, 'If you believe I am getting messages from Jesus, you will get signs.' And I did." Almost daily at the monastery, he encountered pertinent prayers, music shared between them that touched him, readings, or unusually relevant incidents—all leading ultimately to the conclusion that the work on the shroud they could do together was his real calling. He worried about the hurt he might cause others with the decision, especially "my very Catholic mom." But "I can't tell you how many times that year something happened after Sue and I had talked. . . . By the time that year was up, my heart and conscience *made* me leave."

More personal details can only come from them—or from Joe Marino. Sue died in the spring of 2009. But in terms of shroud study, a partnership, destined to be fruitful, was forged. Marino accepted Sue's unorthodox method; she needed and welcomed his shroud expertise.

Together, the two came to a quick realization: what good would it do to solve the mystery of how the image was made if the shroud was believed by most at that time—the eve of the twenty-first century—to be a medieval hoax? Their purpose was not to satisfy certain scientists and historians, or to solve an artistic question. They wanted the shroud vindicated so its spiritual message—that Jesus had lived, died on the cross, and risen again—would be widely heard. Discrediting the Carbon 14 tests, therefore, Sue writes, became their first task.

Initially, Marino confirms, Sue believed some sort of low level radiation from the resurrection had changed the cloth's Carbon 14 content and skewed the tests. Jesus and John were often vague, she wrote, even confusing in their answers to her questions. "As good teachers, they made me work for answers." But after considerable radiation research, she writes, they told her, "You're wrong. The cloth was repaired." It was jarring. She didn't understand. Slowly it dawned on her that maybe the samples were contaminated, not pure linen. She and Marino were aware that since the Raes samples were taken in 1973, there were reports of cotton being in the weave. But, curiously, no one had suggested that because of the reports the sample might be skewed. She asked Marino for pictures of the area from which the Carbon 14 test strip was taken, now available on the internet. This was also the small, discernable corner from which Professor Raes had cut his piece in 1973; in fact, the two (the Raes and later the Carbon 14 cuts) were importantly adjacent. Studying the photos, Sue began to realize that certain threads and aspects of the weave appeared different from those nearby. Had there been a patch? She thought she saw a seam. "If you did not know what you were looking for," she wrote, "you certainly would not see it."

They decided to send the picture of the area to three different textile experts, without telling the experts what the photo showed—namely, the shroud. "Sure enough," she writes, "they all saw discernible differences." One, a "French tailor," said he recognized an "invisible" mending technique "that his European ancestors used to mend damaged linens." In modern times, he said, the mending was known as "in weaving." A skilled medieval weaver used identical or near identical fabric, if need be, to weave a patch matching the overall cloth, and then artfully hand weaved the patch into the cloth. Both the reweave and its reattachment are "invisible" to the untrained eye, the textile expert told Sue. She writes, "There was no doubt in the tailor's mind this technique had been used on the linen sample I was showing him."

But there was a problem. The only patching of the shroud they knew of had occurred after the 1532 fire. (The damaged areas were patched in 1534.) Those patches were large and clearly visible. Then, in historian Ian Wilson's 1998 book *The Blood and the Shroud* (if not other sources), Benford and Marino read in the rear "Chronology" section that, in 1508, Margaret of Austria, the Duchess of Savoy, owner of the relic then, had bequeathed a "snippet of the shroud...to her beloved church of Brou." This was to happen upon her death. She died in 1530 (or 1531 according to some sources). Had her wish been fulfilled?

The more Benford and Marino dug into the matter, the more they believed it had. The corner area in which they saw the differences was 5 $1/2$ by 3 $1/2$ inches—certainly a "snippet" compared to the overall 14-foot long shroud. Prof. Giovani Riggi, who had cut the adjacent C-14 sample, had written in a 1988 Italian publication (*Rapporto Sindone*) that "fibers of other origin" in the sample were "mixed up with the original fabric." Dr. Alan Adler, a chemist and member of STURP, had himself said he believed the area cut for the Carbon 14 sample had been repaired and was not representative of the rest of the shroud. A scientist named Ronald Hatfield at Beta Analytic, the world's largest radiocarbon dating lab, wrote that mixed material like that which they believed the shroud contained (cotton from the sixteenth century and linen 2,000 years old) would return a 1210 AD date of origin, very close to the mean date of 1200 AD given by the three labs testing in 1988.

Benford and Marino wrote this and more in a sourced paper entitled "Evidence for the Skewing of the C-14 Dating of the Shroud of Turin Due to Repairs" and presented it to scientists at the Sindone 2000 Worldwide Congress in Orvieto, Italy. Barrie M. Schwortz, STURP's official documenting photographer and founder of www.shroud.com, the oldest and most visited shroud site on the Internet, was there. "I was listening. It was hard to stay awake with all the distractions of beautiful Italy outside and the same old stuff being presented. All of a sudden Joe and Sue get up there and, wait a minute, I'd never heard this before. Every theory in the world had been proposed [to negate the Carbon 14 datings]—a bioplastic coating [on the shroud], heat from the fire, whatever. All ultimately rejected except by a few. By the time their presentation was over, I'm going, my God, this is the first credible, easy-to-understand explanation that does not require a miracle or some unknown science. I was excited."

After the presentation, Schwortz asked Benford and Marino if he could post their paper on his website. They happily agreed. Other than that, there was little enduring interest in it. But after posting the paper, Schwortz said he got a phone call from his long-time friend, Raymond N. Rogers, one of the original STURP organizers, a distinguished and professionally well-known, retired fellow of Los

Alamos National Laboratory, New Mexico. Schwortz had long before nicknamed Rogers "the gunfighter" for his quick shoot-downs of anything he considered unscientific. "And boy was he angry," Schwortz remembers. The former navy radar technician and Los Alamos explosives expert demanded, "What kind of junk are you putting on your website? These people aren't even scientists! They're part of the lunatic fringe"—a name he gave to "shroudies" who, despite the Carbon 14 dating results (which Rogers accepted), continued to discredit the tests for reasons Rogers thought unscientific. Schwortz says he retorted, "Ray, that's true. But look who they went to—real experts, qualified textile people all of whom agreed there was something anomalous [on the shroud corner]. He was outraged. He said, 'I can prove them wrong in five minutes.' I said, 'Ray, why don't you do it?'"

A SCIENTIST CHALLENGES

Rogers, who had done top secret weapons research at Los Alamos, gladly accepted the challenge. Around the end of 1979, he had received fourteen strands of the Raes sample from Professor Luigi Gonella, the Italian physicist and Turin advisor who had aided STURP as a translator in 1978 and who helped cut the Carbon 14 sample in 1988. Knowing the Raes sample was adjacent to the carbon test cut, and, in fact, threaded into it in places—and was therefore representative of both—Rogers got the strands out and put them under a high-powered microscope. As he began poking them under the lens, he was startled to see clearly distinguishable cotton fibers begin appearing amongst the linen fibers. They had been spliced in. The cotton strands were "easy" to spot, he wrote in a 2002 co-authored paper, entitled "Scientific Method Applied to the Shroud of Turin." Under magnification, the strands were "flat" and "tape-like," while linen fibers were round and resembled tiny bamboo shoots. The cotton fibers were numerous. Having inspected the shroud with even more probing technology in 1978, he knew there was no cotton elsewhere interwoven with the linen.

Reexamining the 1978 ultraviolet and X-ray photos, Rogers now noted with interest—just as Benford and Marino had—the sample corner. The differences in color and contrast compared with the rest of the shroud stood out. The corner was generally darker and a different color, meaning it was chemically different from the rest. This had always been known, but had not been considered important because it was relatively far from the important images in the center of the cloth.

But now, in view of the cotton content and suspected patch, the differences made crucial sense. The area where the samples were taken was not representative of the rest of the cloth—in other words, testing it would not yield the cloth's true age. And as Rogers peered longer into the microscope, he saw a unique, outer covering or "encrustation" on the unraveled cotton fibers. This brownish coating, like the cotton threading itself, was also, he knew, nowhere else on shroud threads. From the way it was variously and haphazardly encrusted, he could tell it had been applied as a liquid and had flowed down the threads. Chemical analysis showed it was madder root in a gum arabic base—a classic dye mixture. (Madder is a plant whose root is used in making, among other things, dyes. Gum arabic is an acacia plant extract used as a mordant, or binder, for dyes.) Benford and Marino had postulated that since the patch was newer material than the older shroud linen, it had to be dyed in order to blend with the rest. Linen was largely resistant to dye, but cotton absorbed it well— which was why, Rogers decided, he was seeing the bulk of the dye stuck on the cotton threads.

In addition, as he examined the 1978 pictures, he saw what appeared to be an "invisible" seam where Benford and Marino believed the sixteenth-century patch to be—a faint diagonal line running between the Raes sample and the area where the later Carbon 14 sample would be cut. Rogers had seen enough. He called Schwortz back. "It was a couple of hours later," Schwortz recalls. "He was calmed down, less irritated. He basically kind of quietly told me, 'I can't believe it, but I've looked, and I think they're right. I've found a splice [i.e., the cotton]. There's nothing like that anywhere else on the shroud. We have photomicroscopy all over [the cloth] and this is unique. Looks like somebody manipulated that corner—tried to hide the weave.' He was much more sedate at that point than earlier when he was kind of yelling at me."

Rogers had a personal reason to be irritated. The scientist who loved dogs and was an amateur archaeologist was dying of terminal cancer and knew he didn't have long—which put a special urgency into his task. "It was embarrassing to have to agree with [Benford and Marino]," he later told the BBC—not because they were non-scientists, but because of his earlier pro-Carbon test stance. But he felt a duty as a scientist to report what he'd found, and he knew if he wanted to be taken seriously by scientific colleagues he needed independent corroboration. Dr. John L. Brown, formerly of Georgia Tech Research Institute's Energy and Materials Sciences Lab, was a leading forensic chemist—a materials sleuth like Rogers. Rogers sent him some Raes samples and asked his independent opinion. Not only did Brown, using different methods and technology (important for an independent verification), validate what Rogers had found, but he noted in a paper he later wrote—"Miscroscopical Investigation of Selected Raes Threads from the Shroud of Turin"—that where "the weave was tight enough," the dye "did not penetrate." In other words, some threads had been so snug in places that the dye had not reached it—an anomaly indicating the coloring had been applied *after* the patch was weaved. To Brown, this was "obvious evidence of a medieval artisan's attempt to dye a newly added repair [in order] to match the aged appearance of the remainder of the shroud."

Brown's findings were the verification Rogers sought. He was then certain the Carbon 14 had been performed on an unrepresentative portion of the shroud—part of the sixteenth-century patch. In the meantime, he came up with another indication that the relic was older than the Carbon 14 tests indicated. It involved vanillin, the organic compound that gives ordinary vanilla its sweet smell. Vanillin is found in flax, the plant from which linen is made. Vanillin is known to dissipate slowly over centuries. For instance, Dead Sea Scroll wrappings, made of linen and known to be roughly 2,000 years old, have lost all their vanillin—as has the overall shroud, according to STURP's nondestructive 1988 examinations. Because heat, storage conditions, and other variables could influence the vanillin content, that fact about the shroud was largely ignored, especially after the Carbon 14 tests. Now, however, prodded by what he was finding, Rogers tested Raes samples, samples of the Carbon 14 cut sent to him by Professor Gonella in 2003, and pieces of linen backing on the shroud known to have been sewed on in the sixteenth century, and found significant amounts of vanillin in each. "The disappearance of all traces of vanillin" in the image areas of the shroud, combined with it's detection in the suspect corner, he wrote, "indicates a much older age [for the relic] than the radiocarbon laboratories reported."

In January 2005, Rogers's peer-reviewed article on his findings was published in the international thermal sciences journal, *Thermochimica Acta*—one of two scientific publications for which he'd served as editor in his long and distinguished career. "They put him through the ringer," says Schwortz about the rigorous peer review—months of questioning and checking. In the article, Rogers wrote,

> The combined evidence from chemical kinetics, analytical chemistry, cotton content, and pyrolysis/ms [mass spectrometry analysis for dye and other traces] proves that the material from the radiocarbon area of the shroud is significantly different from that of the main cloth. The radiocarbon sample was thus not part of the original cloth and is invalid for determining the age of the shroud.

Pope John Paul II and the Shroud

Pope John Paul II visited Turin in May 1998. During his stay there, he spoke of the shroud in an address:

> The Shroud is a challenge to our intelligence. It first of all requires of every person, particularly the researcher, that he humbly grasp the profound message it sends to his reason and his life. The mysterious fascination of the Shroud forces questions to be raised about the sacred Linen and the historical life of Jesus. Since it is not a matter of faith, the Church has no specific competence to pronounce on these questions. She entrusts to scientists the task of continuing to investigate, so that satisfactory answers may be found to the questions connected with this Sheet, which, according to tradition, wrapped the body of our Redeemer after he had been taken down from the cross. The Church urges that the Shroud be studied without pre-established positions that take for granted results that are not such; she invites them to act with interior freedom and attentive respect for both scientific methodology and the sensibilities of believers.

CONFIRMATION

Benford and Marino were, of course, happy to see the article. They'd had sporadic communication with Rogers, and his article gave new-found veracity to what they had started. But Rogers wasn't through. Even in his last days, he wanted more answers, including how the shroud images had been produced (he believed they were the result of a natural chemical reaction, and not any kind of low-level or miraculous radiation). "I don't believe in miracles," was a constant Rogers refrain. He contacted a Los Alamos colleague, Robert Villarreal, a retired nuclear chemist and former Department of Defense scientist who still did work at the giant lab. Rogers wanted Villarreal to use some of the lab's high tech equipment to test image-formation data he had, and also to analyze more deeply a few of the Raes threads which he sent. "Ray repeatedly asserted to me that he was not concerned whether the Shroud was or was not the burial shroud of Jesus, but if a determination was to be made, it must be scientifically correct," Villarreal wrote (in the abstract of a paper presented at Ohio's Shroud Science Group International Conference in 2008).

But Rogers died on March 8, 2005, before Villarreal could get back to him with any answers. For the next eighteen months, the situation lay fallow. Villarreal was not clear on how to proceed until Schwortz, who had filmed Rogers's last interview on the shroud—at Rogers's request, thus deepening the relationship between the two men—contacted Villarreal, seeking the samples Rogers had sent him. Rogers had not told anyone about sending the sample to Villarreal, but another "insight" by Sue Benford now appears to have come into play.

Rogers's wife had given Schwortz her husband's computer and other pieces of his shroud inquiry. Schwortz said he eventually would have gone through Rogers's computer and probably found out about Villarreal himself. But before doing that, and while consulting with Benford about the missing sample, Benford, he said, had another "insight." She told him she had a "feeling" that the sample was at Los Alamos. "She may even have mentioned the name 'Bob' but I can't be sure about that," Schwortz told me. Sue's insight, along with Schwortz's knowledge of Rogers's filing system, quickly led him to a particular file where he found Villarreal mentioned, along with the fact that Rogers had given him the missing sample. Schwortz called Villarreal who, in turn, was equally happy to hear from Schwortz and asked if he should proceed with the project Rogers had asked him to do. "Of course," Schwortz remembers saying. The go-ahead resulted in still further confirmation of Rogers's findings—and this time, perhaps the strongest confirmation of all.

Given the "OK," Villarreal enlisted the best Los Alamos had to offer—not only the latest technology, but nine of the lab's current scientists and technicians. Using new high-resolution microscopes, a variety of spectroscopy and spectrometry, they found both the cotton in the sample and the "cocoon shaped brown crust" holding the threads together. Informed of the confirmation, Schwortz, in consultation with Benford and Marino, sent Villarreal two additional samples which tested the same. Villarreal outlined the work in a presentation at the Ohio conference in 2008. Saying with authority what many sindonologists by this time were already thinking, Villarreal wrote in the abstract:

> Apparently, the age-dating process [1988 Carbon 14] failed to recognize one of the first rules of analytical chemistry that any sample taken for characterization of an area . . . must necessarily be representative of the whole. . . . Our analyses of the three

thread samples taken from the Raes and C-14 sampling corner showed that this was not the case. What was true for the [corner] was most certainly not true for the whole.

Villarreal, like Rogers, recommended a new dating be conducted.

CHAPTER 19

■■■■■■■

THE LAST
HURDLE

1204–1357: BRIDGING THE GAP

●●●●●●●●●●●●●●●●●●●●●●●●●●●●●●●●●●●●●●●

I*f the history of the shroud* had been documented from
Christ's time to the present, there would be little debate
about its origin. But while a good case can be made for its
existence up to the sacking of Constantinople in 1204 AD, and
its history after surfacing in Lirey, France, in 1357 is well documented, there remains the approximate 150-year gap between its
disappearance in Asia Minor and its reappearance in Europe.
How to connect the dots? One speculation was that the Knights
Templar, that fascinating group of Crusader monks, stole the relic
in the 1204 sacking and secretly brought it back to Europe. But

that was only an educated guess based on circumstantial evidence espoused mainly by sindonologist Ian Wilson—that is, until now.

In an April 5, 2009, article in the Vatican newspaper *L'Osservatore Romano*, Vatican researcher and scholar Barbara Frale announced that she had found hard evidence that the Templars had indeed possessed the shroud in that gap of a century and a half. Not only is Frale a respected Templar scholar—having written, among other pieces, an acclaimed book about the mysterious order, *The Templars: The Secret History Revealed* (2004)—but the fact that her research was announced by the Vatican spokespaper indicates the Holy See, which has remained thus far neutral about the shroud, takes her discovery seriously.

Frale is among the leaders uncovering lost information about the controversial warrior monks who, during the Crusades, guarded Christian travelers from Islamic enemies and, in so doing, rose to great power in Medieval Europe and the Holy Land—so much power that they were eventually toppled. Several years ago, Frale's research in the Vatican archives unearthed a misfiled document, the "Chinon Parchment," which absolved the Templars from the charge of heresy. The charge had plagued the order since before their leaders were burned at the stake in early fourteenth-century Paris—the end of a fierce political struggle between the French king and the Pope. Now Frale says she's

---

Pope Benedict XVI and the Shroud

The Catholic Church has announced another exposition of the shroud of Turin, which will be held from April 10 to May 23, 2010. In announcing this exposition, Pope Benedict XVI said it "will provide an appropriate moment to contemplate that mysterious Face which silently speaks to the hearts of men, inviting them to recognize therein the face of God."

unearthed in restricted Vatican files the trial testimony of a young French Templar, Arnaut Sabbatier, who claims to have venerated a shroud-like cloth in a secret 1287 initiation ceremony.

"He testified that he was taken to a secret place to which only the brothers of the Temple had access," *Discovery News* (April 6, 2009) quotes Frale's article from *L'Osservatore Romano*. "There, he was shown a long linen cloth on which was impressed the figure of a man, and was told to kiss the feet of the image three times." The cloth "described in those records," she told *Discovery*, is "extremely similar to the shroud of Turin." The newly unearthed documents, still unpublished, "appear to solve the puzzle of the shroud's missing years."

If Frale's Vatican-backed announcement holds up, it is strong indication that another major piece of the shroud mystery may be solved. Sindonologists, since the documents are still unseen by non-Vatican scholars and therefore un-vetted by them, are hopeful but cautious. Opponents of the shroud's authenticity suggest Frale's research is a convenient announcement on the eve of a scheduled rare public showing of the relic in Turin, to coincide with Easter 2010. In the meantime, scientists interested in the mysteries of the shroud continue working on a variety of new indications that the relic dates from the time of Christ.

NEW SCIENTIFIC EVIDENCE

Supporting Max Frei, the late Swiss criminologist who said he identified Christ-era pollens from Palestine on the shroud, Dr. Avinoam Danin, professor of Botany at Jerusalem's Hebrew University, says he has found, in enhanced shroud photos, images of many thorn, flower, and leaf parts that grow only in and around Israel, some only in the Jerusalem area. The thorn parts include a thistle known as Gundelia tournefortii, which are mostly around the head and shoulders of the shroud images. Many of the flower remnants, including of chrysanthemums, bean caper, and rock rose, are part of what Danin believes were fresh-picked funeral wreaths or "bouquets." Most bloom only in the spring—some only late in the day—and the fact that they are only "slightly wilted" indicates "entombment took place in March-April," coinciding with the Passover when Jesus was crucified.

"The only area on earth where people could put together non-wilted specimens of these plants [with] the Man of the Shroud is . . . between Jerusalem and Hebron," Danin wrote in "Botany of the Shroud of Turin," a paper he delivered at the 2008 Ohio shroud conference.

There is a cloth in Oviedo, Spain, with blood stains and other fluids, which has been there since at least the twelfth century, and which has a circumstantial history back to centuries close to Christ. It is venerated as Jesus' death veil and has many of the same pollen remnants on it as the shroud, according to Danin and a colleague, Uri Baruch, who serves with him on Israel's Antiquities Authority. While the smaller 2 foot by 3 foot cloth, known as the "Sudarium," has no images like the Turin linen, experiments by Dr. Alan Whanger, an American sindonologist and STURP member who worked with Danin, as well as Spanish researchers, have shown that most of the sudarium's stains align with the shroud face, according to Mark Guscin, a British-born scholar, in "The Sudarium of Oviedo: Its History and Relationship to the Shroud of Turin." The length of the nose, for instance, calculated partly through discharged "pleural oedema fluid" on the face cloth "is exactly the same length as the nose on the image of the Shroud." There is an "exact fit of the stains with the beard on the face." Believed thorn wounds coincide. Citing Dr. Whanger's compilations, Guscin writes, "The frontal stains on the sudarium show seventy points of coincidence with the Shroud, and the rear side

shows fifty. The only possible conclusion is that the Oviedo sudarium covered the same face as the Turin Shroud."

International textile expert Methchild Flury-Lemberg says the
shroud is weaved in a style most used at the time of Christ in
Jerusalem. The former curator of Switzerland's Abegg Foundation
Textile Museum told the PBS documentary "Secrets of the Dead"
that a hem in the shroud is "surprisingly" similar to one found on
a cloth in the Jewish fortress of Masada in the Dead Sea area outside Jerusalem. That cloth dates back to between 40 BC and 73 AD.
The shroud's three-to-one herringbone pattern "was special in
antiquity because it denoted an extraordinary quality," she said.
The German-born specialist has restored ancient cloths throughout Europe, including eleventh-century liturgical vestments, and
the Tunic of Christ in Trier, Germany, venerated as Jesus' coat
before the crucifixion. The herringbone "is present on a 12th Century illustration that depicts Christ's funeral cloth," she told the
series. That is significant "because it shows that the painter was
familiar with Christ's Shroud and . . . recognized the indubitably
exceptional nature of the weave of the cloth." Textile evidence
alone cannot date the cloth, she said. But the shroud "does not
display any weaving or sewing techniques which could speak
against it's origin as a high quality product . . . of the first century."

Other researchers believe particles of dirt on the shroud contain
travertine aragonite limestone which is found mainly, if not exclu-
sively, in ancient tombs in Israel. Several believe there are coins over
the eyes of the man in the shroud, something indicated by early
STURP investigators with their space-age instruments. Some believe
the coins have ancient letters on them indicating they are Roman
Leptons minted in the reign of Pontius Pilate, the Roman governor
who presided over Jesus' trial. Others are reporting ancient Jewish
words on the cloth, a leather phylactery (Jewish prayer aid) pouch
on one of the image's arms, even a blood part called bilirubin in the

stains on the shroud. Bilirubin accumulates in the hemoglobin when one undergoes great physical stress such as Jesus would have experienced during his torture and crucifixion.

The Widow's Mite

Professor Francis Filas saw what he thought were impressions of coins over the eyes of the man in the shroud after making blow-ups of the shroud images for a television production in 1979. Later on, in 1981, he had both eyes analyzed digitally. The images of coins stood out clearly over each eye; over the right eye the letters UCAI could be made out clearly. These letters matched the lettering on the back of a Jewish prutah coin (biblically, the "widow's mite") which Filas owned, and which had been minted c. 29 AD.

While the "coin theory" is still heavily debated, it could provide evidence for a much earlier dating of the shroud.

And so it goes. In 2002 the Turin authorities conducted a secret maintenance session with the shroud. It was labeled "for needed restoration." They are said to have scraped and vacuumed the relic, wetting it with a fine mist, and stretching it with weights to smooth wrinkles. The materials removed from the cloth, like pollen, dirt, and surely blood parts, were supposedly put in bottles, presumably for future testing. But many sindonologists, like anthropologist William Meacham, were outraged, not only at the secrecy concerning care of the relic they deem so important to Christianity, but because they charge the restoration was scientifically reckless, first and foremost by possibly rendering the shroud chemically unable to yield future accurate Carbon 14 tests which many of them hope to see. Meacham was so angered at the authorities that in 2005 he published a book entitled *The Rape of the Turin Shroud: How Christianity's most precious relic was wrongly condemned and violated.* (The title refers to the Carbon 14 tests—which condemned the shroud—and the cleaning of the shroud, which Meacham claims violated it.)

HIDDEN SHROUD IMAGES

But emerging from the controversial session—as has been the case with each new scrutiny—was yet a new shroud mystery. Following the 1532 fire, nuns had sewn a protective backing cloth to the rear of the shroud (called a "Holland" cloth because of its origin in that lowland country). During the restoration, the backing was removed. (Flury-Lemberg was one of the 2002 restorers, and it was during these sessions that she inspected the cloth, leading her to decide the style and hem were likely from the first century.) Photos of the uncovered rear were made, and a new backing sewn on, once again hiding the rear side. Apparently, it was following publication of those photos that Professor Giulio Fanti of Padua University's mechanical engineering school identified "ghostly" (as the BBC report on it termed them) images in the photographs of the back of the shroud. Using sophisticated enhancement instruments, Fanti produced pictures showing "a second face," even aspects of hands, on the reverse side. They match the image on the front. "The body image is very faint and the background not uniform," says the abstract of an article he published about it in *The Journal of Optics* (April 13, 2004). The enhanced photos show a face strikingly similar to the face on the front of the shroud. Fanti also says the images are produced by the same discoloration on the tips of the individual linen fibers as the front image, so they are not the result of any paint or other etching substance seeping through. Thus the implication is that these images were produced in the same undiscovered manner as the image on the front.

Could these images be part of another "snapshot" of the body as it emerged from the cloth?

Scientists and those inclined cringe at that thought. But I am not a scientist. Reality, in my opinion, cannot be explained by science alone. There are realities no test tube or sophisticated detection equipment will ever know. The shroud, I think, is specifically a scientific problem by design. It underlines that there is more to the real world than science can as yet detect; it also indicates that there may—as scientists love to say—be more than science will ever be able to explain. It is true I think, however, that science *will* one day discover that there is a spiritual nature to reality—one that would allow for a "dematerialization" of a human body into pure energy. Halos and ghosts, which have been reported since records began, may be detectable "whiffs" of this larger possible reality. This reality is immaterial rather than material. Physicists today are already uncovering a spiritual nature in the strange world of the atom and its immaterial, elusive parts. If we could venture back and tell cave dwellers that they would one day see live pictures on a box, communicate instantly with people around the world, or fly to the moon, how many would believe it? Yet it has all come to pass. In the same way, the shroud, I believe, is a mystery that will someday be solved by science when dematerialization of the body—an advancement of the same rudimentary process that occurs when energy is turned mysteriously into mass—is understood and accepted by science. By then, just as Newtonian physics has given way to Einsteinian theories, scientists may have a new way of looking at what today is deemed unknowable.

Perhaps the shroud is a last attempt by God—or whatever one thinks rules the universe—to show us that the immaterial world exists. For Christians of whatever denomination who need proof, and for others with a tradition of the afterlife, the shroud is concrete—dare I say scientific—evidence that their belief is correct. There is life after death. The shroud is a picture of it and, to Christians, a picture of their founder and what he endured on their behalf—which, if authentic, is certainly an awesome display of what one who loves might endure for another. To me, the fundamental question to be solved about the shroud is not (as important as it is) how the image was made, which I think will eventually be discovered. Nor is it who the man in the shroud may be (though I think it is Jesus). Given all the evidence so far, and the statistical probabilities of who or what the man in the shroud is, I think it is now up to the doubters to prove it is *not* Jesus—a man whose actual, historical existence is supported by as much, if not more, evidence than, say, Plato or Aristotle, although both these men are universally accepted as historical persons.

Science has now established—to my satisfaction, anyway—first, that the blood on the shroud is real human blood. That it flowed in most cases from a live, tortured body (the stains on the chest corresponding to the Biblically described spear in the side being the major exception—the blood there flowed after death). That the stains hardened onto the linen, in most cases, in undisturbed, "picture-perfect" clots stuck to both the body and the cloth. And further, since the lifting of the cloth would disturb and distort these perfectly bordered clots, the fundamental question to me is: how did the body get out of the shroud without messing the clots?

It seems to me there is only one answer.

So now I put it to the reader: you have heard the questions raised and encountered the answers of a host of experts in many fields. You have learned the history of the shroud, from its uncontested arrival in recorded history during the Middle Ages, to its very probable existence dating back to the time of Christ. You have followed the scientific arguments and discovered that the strange images on the shroud could not have been created by any artist, since no artist in the medieval period could have had the know-how, let alone the reason, to create a strange photographic negative. Further, the image contains unique 3-D information which no artist would be able to duplicate. You have watched the shroud sink back into obscurity, as it has countless times before, after the 1988 Carbon 14 testing, only to rise to prominence again as scientists pointed out that the testing had been performed on a patched area of the cloth which was not representative of the whole. You have read the other telling evidence I have gathered. Now it is up to you to decide for yourself: is the shroud a clever hoax, or is it much more? Is it, perhaps, the actual burial cloth of Christ?

Such a question has obvious philosophical implications beyond, as scientists love to stress, what they can deduce. But if answered in the way most shroud research is heading, the question of authenticity becomes, at least to me, moot. Based on the evidence, it seems not only safe but reasonable to assert that the man pictured in the images on the shroud is the man whom all the evidence is pointing to: the man-God Jesus of Christian tradition, and that he has left the world a proof of his resurrection.

ACKNOWLEDGMENTS

The core of this book, although altered now, was originally written in the early 1970s. At that time, I was indebted to Frs. Rinaldi and Otterbein, discussed in this book, who opened doors for me and pointed me in important directions. Unfortunately, they are no longer with us, but I will always remember their patient and gracious guidance.

Prior to sending that core to Macmillan, where it was published in 1977, Marge Keasler, the wife of John Keasler, a fine writer and friend at the *Miami News*, edited the manuscript. It was my first book, and she provided needed help at that stage. John was actually the reason I wrote the book. We had nearby desks at the *News*. I revered him. So one day when he suggested I ought to write a book about the shroud, about which I'd written some religion columns, I took his advice. In New York, I was lucky to visit Bill Griffin, a senior editor at Macmillan. He not only gave me an advance, but was instrumental in shaping the final manuscript. I will always be indebted to him for launching my book-writing career.

Nearly forty years later I want to thank my longtime agents, Jim and Liz Trupin of JET Literary Associates, for helping enable this revised, expanded, and updated edition. Despite the core, it is really a new book on the shroud with many additional new chapters, a perspective that is more seasoned and conclusive than the first, and many facts about the shroud that were not available when the first was published in 1977. Jim placed the book at Regnery, and both Jim and Liz always saw its value as a continuing story. I hope the book has enough success to justify their past efforts.

At Regnery, I want to thank Harry Crocker for shepherding the book to his board, and all the good people there who do such a fine job of preparing and marketing their books. I certainly felt the results of that with *Target: Patton*, and I look forward to more. Most important I want to thank Mary Beth Baker, my editor at Regnery, for her help and patience in putting this new book together. I appreciated greatly her direction and graciousness, which is hard when dealing with someone else's baby.

Lastly, I want to thank my family—wife Bego, son Robert, and daughter Amaya—for their support in numerous ways. Let's throw little Itxaso ("Chaso") in there too, because I am now a grandfather, and even though she doesn't know it, she is always an inspiration—as is her father, Jeremy, an Army captain serving in Afghanistan as I write this. We are all proud of him and awaiting his safe return.

—Robert K. Wilcox

BIBLIOGRAPHY

Abbott, Walter. "Did Christ Leave a Picture of Himself on the Shroud of Turin?" *The Pilot* (Boston), April 17, 1954.

———. "Shroud, The Holy." *Catholic Encyclopedia,* Supplement II, Seventh Section, vol. XVII, 1957.

———. "The Shroud and the Holy Face." *American Ecclesiastical Review,* vol. CXXXII, 1955.

Accetta, August D., John Jackson, and Kenneth Lyons. "Nuclear Medicine and its relevance to the Shroud of Turin." Available online at: http://www.shroud.com.

———. "H.B. doctor submits Shroud of Turin to scientific method." In *Orange County Register,* October 19, 2007.

Adams, Frank O. *A Scientific Search for the Face of Jesus.* Tuscon, AZ: Psychical Aid Foundation, 1972.

Allen-Griffiths, D. *Whose Image and Likeness?* Nottingham: The J & M Publishing Co., 1964.

Antonacci, Mark. *The Resurrection of the Shroud: New Scientific, Medical and Archeological Evidence.* New York: M. Evans and Company, Inc., 2000.

Barbet, Pierre. *Doctor at Calvary.* New York: P. J. Kenedy & Sons, 1953; New York: Image Books, 1963.

Barclay, Vera. *Face of a King.* Bognor Regis, England: Century Arts Press, 1954.

———. "Holy Shroud—Guidance of Dead Sea Skeletons." *Catholic Herald* (London), March 18, 1960.

———. "On the First reactions to the Photographs of the Holy Shroud." *The Altar Server*, June 1959.

Barnes, P. A. *The Holy Shroud: A Reply to the Rev. Herbert Thurston, S.J.* Dublin: M. H. Gill and Son, Ltd., 1928.

———. "The Crucifixion as Told in the Holy Shroud." *Irish Ecclesiastical Record*, LV (1940).

BBC News. "Turin shroud 'older than thought.'" 31 January 2005. Available online at: http://news.bbc.co.uk/2/hi/4210369.stm.

———. "Plants shed light on Turin Shroud," 3 August 1999. Available online at: http://news.bbc.co.uk/2/hi/science/nature/411366.stm.

Benford, M. Sue. *Strong Woman: Unshrouding the Secrets of the Soul.* Nashville, TN: Source Books, Inc., 2002.

Benford, M. Sue, and Joseph Marino. "New Historical Evidence Explaining the 'Invisible Patch' in the 1988 C-14 Sample Area of the Turin Shroud." 2005. Available online at: http://www.shroud.com/pdfs/benfordmarino.pdf.

———. "Discrepancies in the radiocarbon dating area of the Turin Shroud." *Chemistry Today* 26 (July-August 2008).

———. "Evidence for the Skewing of the C-14 Dating of the Shroud of Turin Due to Repairs." 2000. Presented at the Worldwide Congress "Sindone 2000" at Orvieto, Italy. Available online at: www.shroud.com.

Biema, David Van. "Science and the Shroud." *Time*, 20 April 1998.

Boyles, Andrw. *No Passing Glory*. London: Collins, 1955.

Brown, John L. "Microscopical Investigation of Selected Raes Threads from the Shroud of Turin." Georgia Tech Research Institute, 2005. Available online at: www.shroud.com.

Browne, Malcolm W. "Tests Show Shroud of Turin to Be Fraud, Scientist Hints." *New York Times*, September 22, 1988.

Bucklin, Robert. "The Medical Aspects of the Crucifixion of Our Lord Jesus Christ." *Linacre Quarterly*, February 1958.

———. "The Legal and Medical Aspects of the Trial and Death of Christ." *Medicine, Science, and the Law*, January 1970.

Bulst, Werner. *The Shroud of Turin*. Milwaukee: Bruce Publishing Co., 1957.

Case, T. W. *The Shroud of Turin and the C-14 Dating Fiasco: A Scientific Detective Story*. White Horse Press, 1996.

Chalic, The. Summer 1937 issue of the magazine. Brooklyn: Monastery of the Precious Blood, 1937.

Cheshire, Leonard. *The Face of Victory*. London: Hutchinson, 1961.

———. "I Saw the Face of Christ." London *Daily Sketch*, March 7, 1955.

———. *Pilgrimage to the Shroud*. New York: McGraw-Hill Book Company, 1956.

———. "How Christ Was Crucified." London *Picture Post*, April 9, 1955.

Correll, DeeDee. "Shroud of Turin stirs new controversy." *Los Angeles Times*, 17 August 2008

Danin, Avinoam. "Where Did the Shroud of Turin Originate? A Botanical Quest." *Eretz Magazine* November-December 1997.

———. "Botany of the Shroud of Turin." Conference Papers, Shroud Science Group International Conference. Ohio State University, August 14–17, 2008. Available online at: www.ohioshroudconference.com/papers.htm—SP1.

Doepner, Herman. *The Turin Shroud Speaks*. Unpublished manuscript in the collection of Richard Orareo.

Devan, Donald; Eric Jumper; and John Jackson. "A Scientific Search for the New Images on the Holy Shroud of Turin by Computer Enhancement." Unpublished manuscript.

Fanti, Giulio. "The double superficiality of the frontal image of the Turin Shroud." *Journal of Optics A: Pure and Applied Optics* 6 (June 2004).

Frale, Barbara. *The Templars: The Secret History Revealed*. Maverick House, 2009.

Furlong, Francis P. "Jesus Christ Who Was Crucified." *Linacre Quarterly*, vol. 19, 1952.

Glatz, Carol. "Pope Confirms visit to Shroud of Turin; new evidence on shroud emerges." *Catholic News Service*, July 27, 2009.

Green, Jennifer. "Mythbusting Manuscript." *The Ottawa Citizen*, August 5, 2008.

Green, Maurus. "Enshrouded in Silence." *Ampleforth Journal*, vol. LXXIV, 1969.

Heimburger, Thibault. "Cotton in Raes/Radiocarbon Threads: The example of Raes #7." 2009. Available online at: www.shroud.com.

Humber, Thomas. *The Fifth Gospel: The Miracle of the Holy Shroud*. New York: Pocket Books, 1974.

Hynek, R. W. *Science and the Holy Shroud*. Chicago: Benedictine Press, 1936.

———. *The True Likeness*. New York: Sheed & Ward, 1951.

Jennings, Peter. "Still Shrouded in Mystery." *30 Days in the Church and the World* 7 (November 1988).

Johnson, Kendall. *The Living Aura*. New York, Hawthorn Books, 1975.

Katz, Robert. *The Fall of the House of Savoy*. New York: Macmillan Publishing Co., Inc., 1971.

Kilner, J. W. *The Aura*. New York: Samuel Weiser, 1973.

Krippner, S. and D. Rubin. *The Kirlian Aura*. New York: Doubleday, 1974.

Lowe, David. "Turin Shroud WAS used to bury Jesus." *The Sun* (UK) 10 April 2009.

Mackey, H. B. "The Holy Shroud of Turin." *Dublin Review*, vol. CXXII, 1903.

Mannix, Daniel P. *The History of Torture*. New York: Dell, 1964.

Marino, Joseph and Edwin J. Prior. "Chronological History of the Evidence for the Anomalous Nature of the C-14 Sample Area of the Shroud of Turin." 2008. Available online at: www.shroud.com.

Meacham, William. "The Authentication of the Turin Shroud: An Issue in Archeological Epistemology." *Current Anthropology* 24, no. 3 (June 1983).

———. *The Rape of the Turin Shroud*. Lulu.com, 2005.

Meyer, Karl E. "Were You There When They Photographed My Lord?" *Esquire*, August 1971.

Naber, Hans. *See* Reban, John.

O'Gorman, P. W. "The Holy Shroud of Jesus Christ: New Discovery of the Cause of the Impression." *The American Ecclesiastical Review*, vol. CII, 1940.

———. "The Holy Shroud of Christ: Reply to Arguments Against Its Authenticity." *The Irish Catholic*, December 18 and 25, 1941; January 1, 1942.

O'Rahilly, Alfred. Unpublished manuscript. Espous, NY: Wuenschel Collection.

———. "Jewish Burial." *Irish Ecclesiastical Record*, LVIII (1940).

———. "The Burial of Christ." *Irish Ecclesiastical Record*, LVIII (1940) and LIX (1941).

Ostling, Richard N. "Debunking the Shroud of Turin." *Time*, 24 October 1988.

Ostrander, Sheila, and Lynn Schroeder. *Psychic Discoveries Behind the Iron Curtain*.

Otterbein, Adam. "Shroud, Holy." *The New Catholic Encyclopedia*, New York, 1967.

Owen, Richard. "Knights Templar hid the Shroud of Turin, says Vatican," *The Times* (London), 6 April 2009.

Parker, Shafer. "The Shroud of Turin: Latest Research Bolsters Authenticity." *National Catholic Register*, 2002.

Proszymiski, Kazimir de. *The Authentic Photograph of Christ*. London: Search Publishing Co., 1932.

Reban, John (Naber, Hans). *Inquest on Jesus Christ—Did He Die on the Cross?* London: Leslie Frewin, 1967.

Rinaldi, Peter M. "The Holy Shroud." *Sign*, vol. XIII, 1934.

———. *I Saw the Holy Shroud*. Tampa, Florida: Don Bosco Messenger, 1938.

———. "I Saw the Holy Shroud." *Sign,* vol. LIII, February 1974.

———. *It Is the Lord*. New York: Vantage Press, 1972; New York: Warner Paperback Library, 1973.

Rogers, Raymond N. "Studies on the radiocarbon sample from the shroud of Turin." *Thermochimica Acta*, January 2005.

Rogers, Raymond N. and Anna Arnoldi. "Scientific Method applied to the Shroud of Turin, A Review." 2002. Available online at: http://www.shroud.com/pdfs/rogers2.pdf.

Sandhurst, B. G. *The Silent Witness*. Unpublished manuscript from the collection of the Reverend Maurus Green, O.S.B.

Sava, Anthony. "The Blood and Water from the side of Christ." *The American Ecclesiastical Review*, vol. CXXXVIII, 1958.

———. "The Wound in the Side of Christ." *Catholic Biblical Quarterly*, vol. XVI, 1957.

Schneider, Ray. "Unwrapping the Shroud: New Evidence." Available online at: http://www.shroud.com/pdfs/review01.pdf.

Schonfield, Hugh. Preface to Kazimir de Proszymski's *The Authentic Photograph of Christ*. London: Search Publishing Co., 1932.

Stevenson, Kenneth E. and Gary R. Habermas. *Verdict on the Shroud: Evidence for the Death and Resurrection of Jesus Christ*. Ann Arbor, MI: Servant Books, 1981.

Sullivan, Barbara M. "How in Fact Was Jesus Laid in the Tomb?" *National Review*, July 20, 1973.

Thurston, Herbert. "The Holy Shroud as a Scientific Problem." *The Month*, vol. CI, 1903.

——. "The Problem of the Holy Shroud." *The Irish Ecclesiastical Record*, vol. XXIV, 1919.

Vignon, Paul. *The Shroud of Christ*. New Hyde Park, NY: University Books, 1970.

—— and Edward Wuenschel. "The Problem of the Holy Shroud." *Scientific American*, vol. XCIII, 1937.

Walsh, John. *The Shroud*. New York: Random House, 1963.

Weatherhead, Leslie D. *The Manner of the Resurrection*. Nashville, TN: Abingdon Press, 1959.

Weyland, Peter. *A Sculptor Interprets the Holy Shroud of Turin*. Esopus, NY: The Holy Shroud Guild, 1954.

Willis, David. "Did He Die on the Cross?" *Ampleforth Journal*, vol. LXXIV, 1969.

——. "False Prophet and the Holy Shroud." *The Tablet*, June 13, 1970.

Wilson, Ian. "A Gift to Our Proof-demanding Era?" *Catholic Herald* (London), November 16, 1973.

Wuenschel, Edward A. "The Holy Shroud of Turin." *Perpetual Help*, vol. XIII, 1956. This article also appeared, in condense form, in *Catholic Digest*, vol. XIV, 1950.

——. "The Holy Shroud of Turin: Eloquent Record of the Passion." *American Ecclesiastical Review*, vol. XCIII, 1935.

——. "The Holy Shroud: Present State of the Question." *American Ecclesiastical Review*, vol. CII, 1940.

——. "The Photograph of Christ." *Pax*, XV (1937).

——. "The Holy Shroud and Art." *Liturgical Arts*, IX (1941).

——. *Self-portrait of Christ: The Holy Shroud of Turin*. Esopus, NY: The Holy Shroud Guild, 1954.

————. "The Shroud of Turin and the Burial of Christ." *The Catholic Biblical Quarterly*, vol. VII, 1945; vol. VIII, 1946.

————. "The Truth About the Holy Shroud." *American Ecclesiastical Review*, vol. CXXIX, 1953.

http://www.shroud.com, the excellent website run by Barrie Schwortz, STURP photographer. A repository for virtually everything ever written about the shroud, especially modern scientific studies.

http://www.shroudstory.com/, another fine and comprehensive shroud website run by Dan Porter, who has a gift for presenting scientific shroud information to the lay public, including journalists.

www.shroudofturin.com—STURP co-founder John Jackson's website, where the article "The Shroud and Modern Science" can be found, as well as other pertinent shroud information.

INDEX